BECOME WHAT YOU ARE

# Become
# What You Are

## Alan Watts

SHAMBHALA
BOSTON & LONDON
2003

Shambhala Publications, Inc.
Horticultural Hall
300 Massachusetts Avenue
Boston, Massachusetts 02115
*www.shambhala.com*

19  18  17  16  15  14

Printed in the United States of America

⊗ This edition is printed on acid-free paper that meets the
American National Standards Institute z39.48 Standard.

♻ This book is printed on 30% postconsumer recycled paper.
For more information please visit www.shambhala.com.

Distributed in the United States by Penguin Random House LLC
and in Canada by Random House of Canada Ltd

Library of Congress Cataloging-in-Publication Data

Watts, Alan, 1915–1973.
Become what you are/Alan Watts.—Expanded ed.
p.  cm.
ISBN 978-1-57062-940-2
1. Philosophy, Asian.   2. Asia—Religion.   I. Title.
B121.W377 2003
181—dc21
2002026911

# Contents

CONTENTS

# Editor's Preface

AS THE TITLE SUGGESTS, *BECOME WHAT YOU ARE* is a collection of Alan Watts's writings that touch on the dilemma of the person who seeks his or her true self, a quest so often undertaken at the expense of seeing one's life "just as it is." As Alan Watts wrote:

> Life exists only at this very moment, and in this moment it is infinite and eternal. For the present moment is infinitely small; before we can measure it, it has gone, and yet it persists forever. This movement and change has been called Tao by the Chinese. . . . A sage has said that if we *try* to accord with it, we shall get away from it. But he was not altogether right. For the curious thing is that you cannot get out of accord with it even if you want to; though your thoughts may run into the past or the future they cannot escape the present moment.

Understood in this way, to "become what you are" is at once an impossible directive and an unavoidable fact.

This volume is a collection of Alan Watts's articles from the mid-fifties, interspersed with short essays from the late thirties, written before he came to America from England. The shorter pieces appeared originally in *The Middle Way*, a journal published by the Buddhist Lodge of London. The collection begins with "The Paradox of Self-Denial." Although the original manuscript is not dated, the typewriter used to write this piece was acquired in 1953, and the content and length are consistent with other articles that were originally read aloud by Watts on KPFA radio in Berkeley, California, beginning in 1955. These broadcasts were quite popular, and continued for over thirty years.

The second chapter, and the first of the short essays, is the title piece of this volume, and was taken from a scrapbook of Watts's early articles. An examination of the back of the clipping reveals the announcement of meetings of The Buddhist Lodge in March, April, and May of 1938.

The third chapter, "The Finger and the Moon," was retitled thus in Watts's hand, having originally been titled "The Realm of the Spirit." It is dated April 17, 1955, and addresses the shortcomings of Western religious practice in the context of Zen and Asian thought generally. Then, in chapter four we return to the *Middle Way* essays with "Importance," a beautiful little piece on the perspective of a Buddhist poem.

In "Tao and Wu-wei," the fifth chapter, Watts writes about the significance of "not-doing" and "not-forcing," ideas central to Chinese Taoism. Midway through the original text he mentions "these two years of talks," referring to the initial public radio series. This probably was one of the later talks in that series, and his handwritten revisions in the last four pages of the original suggest that this article may have been transcribed from a recording, making it perhaps one of his first broadcasts not read from a script but originally performed before a live radio audience.

"Walking on the Wheel," the sixth chapter, is again a short essay from *The Middle Way*. Here we find Chuang-tzu's "perfect man" as he "walks the wheel" undisturbed by desire, attachment, fear, or regret. On the back side of this clipping we find an interesting quote attributed to Tan Ching, which reads:

———

> If we allow our thoughts, the past, the present and the future ones, to link up in a series, we put ourself under restraint. On the other hand, if we let our mind attach to nothing at all times and towards all things we gain emancipation.

Since Watts was then the editor of *The Middle Way* he probably selected the quote for publication. A similar theme was developed throughout his later works, and the quote serves as evidence of the philosophical influences shaping his thinking at the time.

The seventh chapter marks our departure from the radio articles to an article written for *The Journal of Religious Thought*, published in 1953 by Howard University, in Washington, D.C. "The Language of Metaphysical Experience" is an excellent analysis of the similarities between the knowledge gained by mystical experience and natural science and the linguistic problems posed by expressing that variety of knowledge in words. The article is in many ways far ahead of its time, blending Eastern thought, physics, and Western philosophy and religion toward an understanding of life rooted in wonder, for, as he quotes Goethe:

> the highest to which man can attain is wonder; and if the prime phenomenon makes him wonder, let him be content; nothing higher can it give him, and nothing further should he seek for behind it; here is the limit.

Following "The Language of Metaphysical Experience" we begin a series of articles from *The Middle Way*, including "Good Intentions," "Zen," "The One," "Is There an Unconscious?" "That Far-Off, Divine Event," "The Parable of the Cow's Tail," and "The Second Immortal." The Zennist perspective of Watts's early contribution to *The Middle Way* is fairly represented in the group, followed by the much more serious treatment of Buddhism in "The Problem of Faith and Works in Buddhism." The *Middle Way* selections (later collected in *The Modern Mystic*) conclude with two more short pieces, with "Tomorrow Never

Comes" and "What Is Reality?" and introduce another longer piece from that period. "The Birth of the Divine Son: A Study of a Christian Symbol" was originally published in *The Sufi* in the late thirties. This is an interesting piece in which Watts delves into the mystical basis of the Christian tradition and compares the symbolism of its divinity with those of other religions more often recognized for their mystical nature. As he writes:

> To receive the universe into oneself, after the manner of some "mystics," is simply to become inflated with the conceit that one is God and so set up yet another opposition between the mighty whole and the degraded part. To give oneself utterly and slavishly to the world is to become a spiritual nonentity, a mechanism, a shell, a leaf blown by the winds of circumstance. But if the world is received and the self given at the same time, there prevails that union which brings about the Second Birth.

This rings with familiarity of the Buddhist idea of the Middle Way, as of course it should, and Watts continues along this line of thought concluding in a somewhat Taoist vein:

> Thus when we say that out of the union between self and life (or the world) there is born the Christ, we mean that man rises to a new center of consciousness which is neither himself alone or the world alone. . . . Indeed, this center already exists whether he knows it or not, for no two opposites can exist unless there is a relation between them.

MARK WATTS
*San Anselmo, California*

BECOME WHAT YOU ARE

# The Paradox of Self-Denial

While living, be a dead man, thoroughly dead;
Then, whatever you do, just as you will, will be right.

A BUDDHIST POEM, WRITTEN IN CHINA SEVERAL centuries ago, tries to find words for an intuition which is common to almost every culture in the world. When translated into the familiar language of the Christian tradition, it is so well-known as to be almost a platitude: "He that loseth his soul shall find it." But what always preserves this thought from banality—from the mere tiresomeness of those precepts which everyone knows he ought to observe but doesn't—is that this is a saying which no one *can* observe. For so long as there is something which I can do about it, I am not yet dead; I have not yet completely lost my life. Yet this is not the simple absurdity of a command impossible to obey. It is a real communication, a description of something which happens to people—like the rain, or the touch of the wind. It is simply the expression of the universal discovery that a man does not really begin to be alive until he has lost himself, until he has released the anxious grasp which he normally holds upon his life, his property, his reputation and position. It is the irreducible truth in the monkish idea of "holy poverty," of the way of life to which there are no strings attached, in which—because all is lost—there is nothing to lose, in which there is the exhilaration of a kind of freedom which is poetically likened to the birds and the wind, or to clouds drifting in the boundless sky. It is the life which Saint Paul described as "poor but making many rich, as having nothing but possessing all things."

What an unrealistic nostalgia we have for it! Marie Antoinette playing shepherdess in the gardens of Versailles . . . presidents of great corporations retreating to lonely fishing shacks in the High Sierra . . . the insurance clerk walking alone on the interminable ocean sands, wondering if he would have the courage to be a beachcomber . . . or the moral idealist, reproaching himself because he does not have quite the strength to abandon a comfortable salary and plunge into the slums, like Peter Maurin and Dorothy Day, or the great exemplars Saint Francis and Saint Vincent de Paul. But most of us know that we will not, and probably cannot do it—that we shall continue to cling to our habitual ways of life with all the helplessness of addicts to a destroying passion.

If this begins to sound like a sermon, I do not mean it that way, for I said at the beginning that the words about finding one's life through losing it were not really a precept that could simply be practiced and obeyed. This is what makes all the talk about the necessity of selflessness or the task of transcending the ego so fantastically misunderstood. Treated as a precept, it makes for every kind of moral and spiritual phoniness. Always have a large pinch of salt handy when you meet the fellow who talks about trying to renounce himself, to overcome his ego. I am reminded of the apocryphal conversation between Confucius and Lao-tzu, when the former had been prating of universal love without the element of self.

"What stuff!" cried Lao-tzu. "Does not universal love contradict itself? Is not your elimination of self a positive manifestation of self? Sir, if you would cause the world not to lose its source of nourishment: there is the universe, its regularity is unceasing; there are the sun and moon, their brightness is unceasing; there are the stars, their groupings never change; there are the birds and beasts, they flock together without varying; there are trees and shrubs, they grow upward without exception. Like these, accord with the Tao—with the way of things—and be perfect. Why, then, these vain struggles after charity and duty to one's neighbor, as though beating a drum in search of a fugitive. Alas, sir, you have brought much confusion into the mind of man!"

As I said, the truth about finding life through losing it is not a precept but a report of something which happens—and happens in many different ways. It is not given to everyone to be an obvious moral hero or a notorious saint. It is not everyone's way to be a rolling stone without the responsibilities of wife and children. Nor, I should add, is it everyone's privilege to be a self-sacrificing wife or model husband. And still more—it is not everyone's gift to be the contented fatalist, accepting himself and his limitations just as they are, knowing that he is a weed and not trying to be a rose. Some of us will always be trying—with an exasperating degree of relative success—to improve ourselves in one way or another, and no amount of self-acceptance will stop it. Self-renunciation, self-acceptance—these are all names for the same thing, for the ideal to which there is no road, the art for which there is no technique.

Why, then, does this whole idea so commonly wear the form of a precept, of advice to be followed, of a method to be applied? For obviously there is a vital contradiction in the very notion of self-renunciation, and just as much is self-acceptance. People try to accept themselves in order to be different, and try to surrender themselves in order to have more self-respect in their own eyes—or to attain some spiritual experience, some exaltation of consciousness the desire for which is the very form of their self-interest. We are really stuck with ourselves, and our attempts to reject or to accept are equally fruitless, for they fail to reach that inaccessible center of our selfhood which is trying to do the accepting or the rejecting. The part of our self that wants to change our self is the very one that needs to be changed; but it is as inaccessible as a needle to the prick of its own point.

But the reason why the idea of self-renunciation appears in the impossible form of a precept is that it is a form of what Buddhists would call *upaya*—a Sanskrit term meaning "skillful means," and more particularly the skillful means employed by a teacher to awaken his student to some truth which can only be reached in a roundabout way. For the selfishness of the self thrives on the notion that it can command itself, that it is the lord and master of its own processes, of its own motives and desires. Thus the one important result of any really serious attempt at self-renunciation or self-acceptance is the humiliating discovery that it is impossible. And this precisely is that death to oneself which is the improbable source of a way of life so new and so alive that it feels like having been born again. In this metaphorical sense, the ego dies on finding out its own incapacity, its inability to make any difference to itself that is really important. That is why, in Zen Buddhism, the task of self-transcendence is likened to a mosquito trying to bite an iron bull, and, in the words of one of the old masters, the transforming death comes about at the very moment when the iron hide of the bull finally and absolutely rejects the mosquito's frail proboscis.

There is, of course, still some refuge for our illusion of self-importance in the idea that we must first make a very resolute effort to bite the bull. Every "in-group" distinguishes itself from the "out-group," the initiates from the hoi polloi, by some process of "going through the mill," of enduring sufferings which are subsequently worn as the proud badge of graduation. Thus one of the more sickening aspects of spiritual phoniness is the usually rather subtly hinted implication that one has, after all, "suffered so much." So, too, in the person who is still a mere aspirant to the state of grace, the same kind of humbug wears the form of resolutions to bite the bull to the utmost—in order to have oneself finally and effectively convinced that it cannot be done.

I have always found that the people who have quite genuinely died to themselves make no claims of any kind to their own part in the process. They think of themselves as lazy and lucky. If they did anything at all, it was so simple that anyone else could do the same—for all that they have done is to recognize a universal fact of life, something as true of the weak and foolish as of the wise and strong. They would even say that in this respect there is some advantage in being weak and foolish, for the possession of a strong will and a clever head makes some things very difficult to see. A successful merchant will perhaps be less ready than a mere tramp to see that the same oblivion engulfs both of them. To the genuine dead-man-come-alive, sage, mystic, buddha, *jivanmukta*, or what you will, the notion that he attained this state by some effort or by some special capacity of his own is always absurd and impossible.

You may almost be sure, then, that some kind of clericalism, some kind of highly refined spiritual racket, is at work when stress is laid upon the suffering and the discipline, the endurance and the willpower, which are said to be the essential prerequisites of an entry to the kingdom of heaven. Such talk is sometimes just making the best of a bad job—trying to pretend to oneself that a life of constant self-frustration was in fact a great spiritual attainment. Sometimes it may simply be an honest mistake, for there are people who discover what was always close at hand only after a long and painful journey, and they remain under the impression that the most awkward road was the only road. Sometimes, however, talk of this kind is the really nasty kind of preaching affected by people who presume to be schoolmasters to their fellow man. But their sermons never have the slightest creative effect, since the only motives for action which they supply are shame or fear or guilt, and when we respond to such motives we find only a balm for the ego's injured pride—a balm upon which our egocentricity flourishes with special gusto.

With such misunderstandings out of the way, perhaps we can consider more intimately what it means to find life by losing it. The main point is, I think, that the state metaphorically called death or self-surrender is not a future condition to be acquired. It is rather a present fact. In small matters, our ego shows some signs of life. But fundamentally, in the presence of great space and time, as of great love and great fear, we are leaves on the wind. When we begin to think about this clearly, we evoke very disturbing emotions, which we would like to be able to control. Our resistance to these emotions is as natural as the emotions themselves. Indeed, they are really the same as the emotions, since emotions appear only as manifestations of a state of tension and resistance. If I did not dislike fear, it would not be fear. Nevertheless, there is, I think, no difficulty in discovering that our resentment of those emotions, our unwillingness to experience them, is totally ineffectual. It is the mosquito biting the iron bull again. The fragility and frailty of our human bodies within the merciless and marvelous torrent of life evokes every emotion of this agonizingly sensitive organism—love, anger, sadness, terror, and the fear of terror. And our attempts to stand above these emotions and control them are the emotions themselves at play, since love is also to be in love with love, and sadness to be sorry that one is sad. Our unwillingness to feel is the very measure of our ability to feel, for the more sensitive the instrument, the greater its capacity for pain, and so for reluctance to be hurt.

Now, there are some psychologists who have struck, rather clumsily perhaps, upon an important truth—namely that there is a serious mistake in not responding to our feelings, or in trying to feel in some other way than we feel actually. They are speaking here, it should be noted, of inward feelings, and not of overt action. In other words, if you, as a mother, hate your child, don't try to pretend to yourself that you love him. But—put in this rather oversimplified way—this insight degenerates into another precept: "Accept your feelings: go along with your emotions." It is not that simple, because our feelings conflict with one another—as for example, when we are too proud to cry, or too frightened to fall in love. In this case, which feeling do we accept—the sorrow or the pride, the fear or the love?

Now, this is a most instructive example of the difficulty of self-acceptance, for in such a situation we find that we can accept neither. The conflict will not allow itself to be resolved by a decision for one of the two sides—and we are stuck, helplessly, with the conflict.

But the real importance of what these psychologists are trying to say is that there is an almost uncanny wisdom in the spontaneous and natural reactions of our organism to the course of events. The extraordinary capacity to feel an event inwardly, as distinct from bursting into precipitate action to avoid the tension of feeling—this capacity is in fact a wonderful power of adaptation to life, not unlike the instant responses of flowing water to the contours of the ground over which it flows. I hope this is clear. I am not talking at the moment of responses in terms of action, but only of our inward, subjective responses of feeling. The point is that our feelings are not really a kind of resistance, a kind of fight with the course of events. They are a harmonious and intelligent response. A person who did not feel frightened at the threat of danger would be like a tall building with no "give" to the wind. A mind which will not melt—with sorrow or love—is a mind which will all too easily break.

Now, the reason why I am talking of feeling rather than outward action is that I am considering the predicament of man in the face of events about which nothing can be done—events toward which our sole response is a response of feeling. I am thinking of the ultimate certainty of death, the overall helplessness of man within the vast tide of life, and, finally, of the very special feelings which arise when we are faced with a conflict of feelings which cannot be resolved. All these situations evoke feelings which, in the long run, are as irresistible as the situations themselves are insoluble. They are the ultimate feelings—and much of what is called philosophy is the fruitless attempt to talk oneself out of them.

Thus what I have called the death of the ego transpires in the moment when it is discovered and admitted that these ultimate feelings are irresistible. They are ultimate in two senses: one, that they sometimes have to do with very fundamental and cataclysmic events, and, two, that they are sometimes our deepest, most radical feeling with respect to a given situation—such as the basic frustration provoked by a conflict between sorrow and shame. The point is that these ultimate feelings are as wise as all the rest, and their wisdom emerges when we give up resisting them— through the realization that we are simply unable to do so. When, for example, life compels us at last to give in, to surrender to the full play of what is ordinarily called the terror of the unknown, the suppressed feeling suddenly shoots upward as a fountain of the purest joy. What was formerly felt as the horror of our inevitable mortality becomes transformed by an inner alchemy into an almost ecstatic sense of freedom from the bonds of individuality. But ordinarily we do not discover the wisdom of our feelings because we do not let them complete their work; we try to suppress them or discharge them in premature action, not realizing that they are a process of creation which, like birth, begins as a pain and turns into a child.

I hope it is possible to say all this without tying it up with the atmosphere of "ought-ness," without giving anyone the notion that this kind of self-surrender is something which one should or can do. This willful, compulsive, moralistic approach to man's transformation always obstructs it—for it still implies that very illusion of self-mastery which stands in the way. But it is just when I discover that I *cannot* surrender myself that I am surrendered; just when I find that I cannot accept myself that I am accepted. For in reaching this hard rock of the impossible one reaches sincerity, where there can no longer be the masked hide-and-seek of I and Me, "good I" trying to change "bad Me," who is really the same fellow as "good I." In the expressive imagery of Zen, all this striving for self-surrender is like trying to put legs on a snake—or, shall I say, like a naked man trying to lose his shirt. To quote from that genial Taoist, Chuang-tzu: From the standpoint of the sage, "the joined is not united, nor the separated apart, nor the long in excess, nor the short wanting. For just as a duck's legs, though short, cannot be lengthened without pain to the duck, and a crane's legs, though long, cannot be shortened without misery to the crane—so that which is long in man's moral nature cannot be cut off, nor that which is short be lengthened."

# Become What You Are

IT HAS BEEN SAID THAT THE HIGHEST WISDOM
lies in detachment, or, in the words of Chuang-tzu: "The perfect
man employs his mind as a mirror; it grasps nothing; it refuses
nothing; it receives, but does not keep." Detachment means to
have neither regrets for the past nor fears for the future; to let life
take its course without attempting to interfere with its movement
and change, neither trying to prolong the stay of things pleasant
nor to hasten the departure of things unpleasant. To do this is to
move in time with life, to be in perfect accord with its changing
music, and this is called Enlightenment. In short, it is to be detached from both past and future and to live in the eternal Now.
For in truth neither past nor future have any existence apart from
this Now; by themselves they are illusions. Life exists only at this
very moment, and in this moment it is infinite and eternal. For
the present moment is infinitely small; before we can measure it,
it has gone, and yet it persists for ever. This movement and
change has been called Tao by the Chinese, yet in fact there is no
movement, for the moment is the only reality and there is nothing beside it in relation to which it can be said to move. Thus it
can be called at once the eternally moving and eternally resting.

How can we bring ourselves into accord with this Tao? A sage
has said that if we *try* to accord with it, we shall get away from it.
But he was not altogether right. For the curious thing is that you

cannot get out of accord with it even if you want to; though your thoughts may run into the past or the future they cannot escape the present moment. However far back or forward they try to escape they can never be separated from the moment, for those thoughts are themselves of the moment; just as much as anything else they partake of, and, indeed, *are* the movement of life which is Tao. You may believe yourself out of harmony with life and its eternal Now; but you cannot be, for you are life and exist Now—otherwise you would not be here. Hence the infinite Tao is something which you can neither escape by flight nor catch by pursuit; there is no coming toward it or going away from it; it *is*, and you are it. So become what you are.

# The Finger and the Moon

---

THERE IS AN OLD CHRISTIAN PHRASE—*Crux medicina mundi*—the Cross, the medicine of the world—a phrase which is rather remarkable in that it suggests that religion is a medicine rather than a diet. The difference is, of course, that medicine is something to be taken occasionally—like penicillin—whereas a diet is regular food. Perhaps this analogy cannot be pressed too far, since there are medicines like insulin which some people have to take all the time. But there is a point to the analogy—a point expressed in another Latin saying, not at all Christian, since its author was Lucretius: *Tantum religio potuit suadere malorum* (Too much religion is apt to encourage evil). I am not thinking so much of the exploitation of the poor by a corrupt priesthood, or of the obvious evils of zealotry and fanaticism. I am thinking, rather, of the old Buddhist metaphor of the doctrine which is like a raft for crossing a river. When you have reached the opposite shore, you do not carry the raft on your back, but leave it behind.

There is something here which applies not only to the mere handful of people who might be said to have reached the opposite shore, but to most of us. To carry out the metaphor a little: if you are going to cross the river, you must make haste, for if you dally on the raft, the current will carry you downstream, and out to the ocean—and then you will be stuck on the raft forever. And it is so easy to get stuck—on the raft, on religion, on psychotherapy, on philosophy. To use another Buddhist simile: The doctrine is like a finger pointing at the moon, and one must take care not to mistake the finger for the moon. Too many of us, I fear, suck the pointing finger of religion for comfort, instead of looking where it points.

Now it seems to me that what the finger of religion points at is something not at all religious. Religion, with all its apparatus of ideas and practices, is altogether a pointing—and it does not point at itself. It doesn't point at God, either, for the notion of God is part and parcel of religion. I might say that what religion points at is reality, except that this merely puts a philosophical notion in place of a religious one. And I can think of a dozen other substitutes for God or reality. I could say that it points at one's true Self, at the eternal Now, at the nonverbal world, at the infinite and ineffable—but really none of this is very helpful. It's just putting one finger in place of another. When Joshu asked his teacher Nansen, "What is the Tao, the Way?" Nansen replied, "Your everyday mind is the Tao."

But this doesn't help, either, for as soon as I try to understand what is meant by my everyday mind, and then try to latch on to it, I am just sucking another finger. But why does this difficulty arise? If someone actually points his finger at the moon, I have no difficulty in turning and looking at the moon. But the thing at which these religious and philosophical fingers are pointing seems to be invisible, so that when I turn to look there is nothing there, and I am forced to go back to the finger to see whether I understood its direction correctly. And sure enough, I find time and time again that I made no mistake about its direction—but for all this I simply cannot see what it's pointing at.

All this is equally exasperating for the person who is doing the pointing, for he wants to show me something which, to him, is so obvious that one would think any fool could see it. He must feel as we all feel when trying to explain to a thick-headed child that two times zero is zero and not two, or some other perfectly simple little fact. And there is something even more exasperating than this. I am sure that many of you may, for a fleeting moment, have had one clear glimpse of what the finger was pointing at—a glimpse in which you shared the pointer's astonishment that you had never seen it before, in which you saw the whole thing so plainly that you knew you could never forget it . . . and then you lost it. After this, there may be a tormenting nostalgia that goes on for years. How to find the way back, back to the door in the wall that no longer seems to be there, back to the turning which led into paradise—which wasn't on the map, which you saw for sure right here. But now there is nothing. It is like trying to trace someone with whom you fell in love at first sight, and then lost touch; and you go back to the original place of meeting again and again, trying in vain to pick up the threads.

If I may put it in a way which is horribly cumbersome and inadequate, that fleeting glimpse is the perception that, suddenly, some very ordinary moment of your ordinary everyday life, lived by your very ordinary self, just as it is and just as you are—that this immediate here-and-now is perfect and self-sufficient beyond any possibility of description. You know that there is nothing to desire or seek for—that no techniques, no spiritual apparatus of belief or discipline is necessary, no system of philosophy or religion. The goal is here. It is this present experience, just as it is. That, obviously, is what the finger was pointing at. But the next moment, as you look again, the instant in which you are living is as ordinary as ever, though the finger still points right at it.

However, this irritatingly elusive quality of the vision to which the finger points has an extremely simple explanation, an explanation which has to do with what I said at the beginning about getting rid of the raft when you have crossed the river, about taking religion as a medicine but not as a diet. For purposes of understanding this point, we must take the raft as representing the ideas or words or other symbols whereby a religion or a philosophy expresses itself, whereby it points at the moon of reality. As soon as you have understood the words in their plain and straightforward sense, you have already used the raft. You have reached the opposite bank of the river. All that remains now is to do what the words say—to drop the raft and go walking on the dry land. And to do this, you *must* drop the raft. In other words, you cannot, at this stage, think about religion and practice it at the same time. To see the moon, you must forget the pointing finger, and simply look at the moon.

This is why all the great Asian philosophies begin with the practice of concentration, that is, of attentive looking. It is as if to say, "If you want to know what reality is, you must look directly at it and see for yourself. But this needs a certain kind of concentration, because reality is not symbols, it is not words and thoughts, it is not reflections and fantasies. Therefore to see it clearly, your mind must be free from wandering words and from the floating fantasies of memory." To this we are probably apt to reply, "Fine, but this is easier said than done." There always seems to be a problem about translating words into action, and this problem seems to be peculiarly acute when it comes to the so-called spiritual life. Faced with this problem, we back up and start to busy ourselves with a lot of discussion about methods, techniques, and other aids to concentration. But it should be simple enough to see that this is nothing but procrastination and postponement. You cannot, at the same time, concentrate and think about concentrating. It sounds almost silly to say it, but the only way to concentrate is to concentrate. In actually doing it, the idea of doing it disappears—and this is the same thing as saying that religion disappears when it becomes real and effective.

Now a great deal of the talk about the difficulty of action, or the difficulty of concentration, is sheer nonsense. If we are sitting down together at a meal, and I say to you, "Please pass the salt"—you just do it, and there is no difficulty about it. You do not stop to consider the right method. You do not trouble yourself with the problem of how, when you have picked the saltshaker up, you are going to be able to concentrate on it long enough to bring it to my end of the table. Now there is absolutely no difference between this and concentrating the mind's attention to see into the nature of reality. If you can concentrate the mind for two seconds, you can do it for two minutes, and if you can do it for two minutes, you can do it for two hours. Of course, if you want to *make* this kind of thing horribly difficult, you begin to think about timing yourself. Instead of concentrating, you begin to think about whether you are concentrating, about how long you have concentrated, and about how much longer you are going to keep it up. All this is totally off the point. Concentrate for one second. If, at the end of this time, your mind has wandered off, concentrate for another second, and then another. Nobody ever has to concentrate for more than one second—this one. This is why it is quite literally off the point to time yourself, to compete with yourself, and to bother about your progress and success in the art. It's simply the old story of making a difficult job easy by taking it one step at a time.

There is, perhaps, another difficulty—and this is that in the state of concentration, of clear unwavering attention, one has no self—that is, no self-consciousness. This is because the so-called self is a construct of words and memories, of fantasies which have no existence in immediate reality. The block or stoppage which so many of us feel between words and action, between symbol and reality is actually a case of wanting to have one's cake and eat it. We want to enjoy *ourselves,* and fear that if we forget ourselves there will be no enjoyment—an entertainment without anyone present to be entertained. This is why self-consciousness is a constant inhibition of creative action, a kind of chronic self-frustration, such that civilizations which suffer from an overdose of it go raving mad, invent atom bombs and blow themselves up. Self-consciousness is a stoppage because it is like interrupting a song after every note so as to listen to the echo, and then feeling irritated because of the loss of rhythm.

This is all really a case of our own proverb, "a watched pot never boils." For if you try to watch your mind concentrate, it will not concentrate. And if, when it is concentrated, you begin to watch for the arrival of some insight into reality, you have stopped concentrating. Real concentration is therefore a rather curious and seemingly paradoxical state, since it is at once the maximum of consciousness and the minimum of ego-feeling, which somewhat gives the lie to those systems of Western psychology which identify the conscious principle with the ego. Similarly, it is the maximum of mental activity or efficiency, and the minimum of mental purposiveness, since one cannot simultaneously concentrate and expect a result from concentration.

The only way to enter into this state is precipitately—without delay or hesitation, just to do it. This is why I ordinarily avoid discussion of all the various kinds of Asian meditation techniques, such as Yoga. For I am inclined to feel that for most Westerners, these are not aids but obstacles to concentration. It is not unaffected and natural for us to assume the lotus posture and go through all sorts of spiritual gymnastics. So many Westerners who do this kind of thing are so self-conscious about it, so preoccupied with the *idea* of doing it that they never really do it at all. For the same reason, I am rather leery of too much Zen—especially when it means importing all the purely incidental apparatus of Zen from Japan, all the strictly technical formalities, and all the endless and pointless discussion about who has or hasn't attained satori, or about how many koans one has solved, or how many hours a day one sits in zazen, or meditation.

This sort of thing is not Zen or Yoga; it is just a fad, just religiosity, and is precisely self-consciousness and affectation rather than unselfconsciousness and naturalness. If, however, you can really do the thing itself—that is, if you can learn to wake up and concentrate at the drop of a hat—you can take or leave the trimmings as you will. For the fear of exoticism should not prevent us from enjoying the really beautiful things which Asian culture has to offer—Chinese painting, Japanese architecture, Indian philosophy, and all the rest. But the point is that we cannot really enter into the spirit of these things at all unless, in the first place, we can acquire the special kind of relaxed concentration and clear-sightedness which is essential for their proper appreciation.

Of themselves, they will not give us that capacity—which is something innate. If you have to import it from Asia, you do not have it at all. Therefore, the important thing is simply to begin—anywhere, wherever you are. If you happen to be sitting, just sit. If you are smoking a pipe, just smoke it. If you are thinking out a problem, just think. But don't think and reflect unnecessarily, compulsively, from sheer force of nervous habit. In Zen, they call this having a leaky mind—like an old barrel with open seams which cannot contain itself.

Well, I think this is enough medicine for tonight. So let's put the bottle away, and go out and look at the moon.

# Importance

BUDDHISM IS OFTEN ACCUSED OF BEING A RELIgion so absorbed in the impersonal and the eternal that it overlooks the importance of individual and temporal things. According to its teaching, all things that have form are subject to change and void of any enduring "self," but this does not imply that such things are unimportant. Importance is not measured by time, and change is a symptom of the presence of life. A Japanese poem says:

> The morning glory blooms for an hour,
> Yet it differs not at heart
> From the giant pine which lives a thousand years.

Beside the immensity of Time and Space, man seems a being of the most utter insignificance. In comparison with the vastly complicated problems of the modern world, the lesser hopes and fears of the individual seem of no consequence. But Buddhism is the Middle Way, and must necessarily regard such an extreme attitude as false philosophy. It is well that one who is too much concerned with his own affairs should consider the immensity of the universe and the destiny of the human race. But let him not consider it too long, lest he forget that the responsibility not only for human prosperity but also for the order of the universe is his own. While modern astronomy tells us of our insignificance beneath the stars, it also tells us that if we lift so much as a finger, we affect them. It is true that we are transient, that we have no abiding self, but the fabric of life is such that one broken thread may work immeasurable ruin. The magnitude of the world with whose destiny we are bound up increases rather than diminishes our importance. Nature may seem to have little regard for individuals; it may let them die in millions as if it mattered nothing. But value is in quality, not quantity. A pea may be as round as the world, but as far as roundness is concerned, neither is better than the other. And man is in himself a little universe; the ordering of his mind and body is as complex as the ordering of the stars. Can we say, then, that the governing of a man's universe is less important because it is different in size?

# Tao and Wu-Wei

The essence of Lao-tzu's philosophy is the difficult art of getting out of one's own way—of learning how to act without forcing conclusions, of living in skillful harmony with the processes of nature instead of trying to push them around. For Lao-tzu's Taoism is the philosophical equivalent of jujitsu, or judo, which means the way of gentleness. Its basis is the principle of Tao, which may be translated the Way of Nature. But in the Chinese language the word which we render as "nature" has a special meaning not found in its English equivalent. Translated literally, it means "self-so." For to the Chinese, nature is what works and moves by itself without having to be shoved about, wound up, or controlled by conscious effort. Your heart beats "self-so," and, if you would give it half a chance, your mind can function "self-so"—though most of us are much too afraid of ourselves to try the experiment.

Other than this, Lao-tzu didn't actually say very much more about the meaning of Tao. The Way of Nature, the Way of happening self-so, or, if you like, the very process of life, was something which he was much too wise to define. For to try to say anything definite about the Tao is like trying to eat your mouth: you can't get outside it to chew it. To put it the other way round: anything you can chew is not your mouth. So, too, anything you can define or imagine, anything you can understand or desire, is not the Tao. We can't know it, we can't feel or sense it, for the very simple reason that it's the whole substance of knowing, feeling, and sensing, of living and existing. It's too close to be seen and too obvious to be noticed or understood. If I may say something which sounds utterly ridiculous, it's more *us* than we are ourselves—more you than you, more I than me. Putting it more clearly, perhaps, it's the you that grows your nervous system, rather than the you that uses the nerves to decide, think, and act. That will do for the moment, even though not quite right. If I try to make it clearer, it will just get more and more complicated.

Now, I believe that almost all human beings make some sort of a distinction between the self that wills and acts, and the subconscious self that manages our hearts and glands and nerves. Such words as self-control and self-consciousness suggest this division of our being into two parts, knower and known, thinker and thoughts. To the degree that we feel this division, we are always trying to control and understand and dominate our subconscious self with our conscious and willful self. But in Lao-tzu's philosophy, this is quite literally to be all balled-up—to be in a desperate and utterly frustrating condition of self-strangulation, falling over one's own feet, and perpetually getting in one's own way—which is, of course, not Tao, the Way of Nature. This is why our principal problem in life is ourselves—why we are so tormented with anxiety about self-preservation and self-control, why we are so mixed up that we have to make laws to regulate our behavior, employ police to keep ourselves in order, and equip armies with explosives to prevent us from blowing ourselves up. In the more intimate sphere of personal life, the problem is the pain of trying to avoid suffering and the fear of trying not to be afraid.

Obviously, anyone who realizes the enormity and absurdity of this predicament wants to get out of it, wants to get un-balled-up, to get back to the uninvolved sanity of the Tao. But this is so much more easily done than said that it's very difficult indeed. For, according to Lao-tzu, the way back, or forward, to harmony with the Tao is, in the profoundest and most radical sense, to do nothing at all. But I said that this was so much more easily done than said, because the moment we begin to talk or think about it, it becomes immensely difficult to understand, to clear from innumerable misinterpretations. In the Chinese language, this special kind of doing nothing is called *wu-wei*—literally, nondoing or nonstriving. This term is perhaps a bit awkward because the Chinese *wei*, to do, sounds rather like the English *way*, so to avoid unnecessary confusion in a confusing subject, I shall pronounce *wu-wei* in the Japanese style—*mui*.

When Lao-tzu said that *mui*, doing nothing, was the secret of harmony with the Tao, he really meant it. But what he meant by it must be distinguished very carefully from two other courses which sound quite different from one another, though they are really the same. The first course, I will call the way of deliberate imitation. This is to suppose that we actually know what the sane and natural way of living is, to embody it in laws and principles, techniques and ideals, and then try by a deliberate effort of imitation to follow them. This leads to all the contradictions with which we are so familiar, the contradiction of man bawling himself out—as well as up—for not doing what he tells himself to do.

The second, and seemingly opposed course, I will call the way of deliberate relaxation, the way of "to hell with it all." This is to try not to control oneself, to attempt to relax one's mind and let it think whatever it wants, to set out to accept one's self as it is without making any effort to change it. This leads to a vast, sloppy, disorganized mess, or to a kind of compulsive stillness, or sometimes to an equally compulsive psychological diarrhea.

Both of these courses are far short of the real *mui*, of profound and radical nondoing. What brings them to the same thing is that, in their different ways, the two courses had a result in mind.

They consisted equally in something done, or not done, to get to a goal. The goal in question was some sort of image, some mental picture, some vague feeling, of an ideal, of a state of accord with the Tao, of harmony with the Way of Nature.

But it was precisely in relation to such notions and ideals that Lao-tzu said: "Get rid of knowledge; eject wisdom, and the people will be benefited a hundredfold." He was talking about supposed knowledge of what the ideal way of life is. As I said at the beginning, there is simply no way of knowing what the Tao is. If we cannot possibly define the Tao, we certainly cannot define what it is to be in harmony with the Tao. We have simply no idea of what the goal ought to be.

If, then, we act, or refrain from action, with a result in mind—that result is not the Tao. We can say, then, that *mui* is not seeking for any result. Of course, this doesn't mean that a Taoist comes to the table without expecting dinner, or gets on a bus to go nowhere special. I am talking of results in the moral and spiritual sphere—such things as goodness, peace of mind, sanity, happiness, personality, courage, and so forth.

Well then, is it possible for me to stop seeking for these results? Surely, the very question implies that I have still a result in mind, even if this is the state of not seeking results. It seems, therefore, that I am helpless, that I am simply unable to think or act without some result in mind. It makes no difference whether I do or don't do: I am still, compulsively, helplessly, seeking a result. So I find myself in a teleological trap. I must purpose. I might almost say, I *am* purpose.

Now this is an immensely important discovery. For it means that I have found out what I, what my ego, actually is—a result-seeking mechanism. Such a mechanism is rather a useful gadget when the results in question are things like food or shelter for the organism. But when the results which the mechanism seeks are not external objects but states of itself, such as happiness, the mechanism is all clutched-up. It is trying to lift itself up by its own bootstraps. It is working purposefully, as it must, but to no purpose. It is looking for results in terms of itself. It wants to get results from the process of looking for results. This is a hopelessly and wildly fouled-up feedback mechanism. There is, however, just this one possibility. It can realize the whole round circuit of the trap in which it lies. It can see the entire futility and self-contradiction of its position. And it can see that it can do nothing whatsoever to get itself out of it. And this realization of "I *can* do nothing" is precisely *mui*. One has mysteriously succeeded in doing nothing.

At this moment, there is a sudden shift in the center of gravity of one's whole personality. You simply *find* yourself outside the trap, outside the result-seeking mechanism, which now appears as a sort of object which has purposes all to no purpose. You see yourself as a purpose-seeking creature, but realize that there is no purpose for the existence of such a creature. In relation to everything except your own preservation, you are marvelously futile. Your aim is to preserve and perpetuate yourself, but in the larger context of the universe there is no reason, no purpose for this aim.

Formerly, this would have depressed you. Now it doesn't bother you at all. For, as I said, the center of gravity has shifted, and you no longer find yourself identified with this absurd mechanism of purposeless purpose. In Lao-tzu's own words: "The universe is everlasting. The reason that the universe is everlasting is that it does not live for itself. Therefore it lasts. Therefore the sage puts himself behind, and finds himself in front, regards his person as outside himself, and his person is preserved. Is it not because he does not live for himself that he realizes himself?" In other words, when the shift has taken place, when he finds himself outside of himself, outside of the teleological trap, the trap unwinds, the result-seeking mechanism straightens out and no longer seeks itself, or states of itself.

But remember, all of this happens *mui*—another good translation of which might be "no-how," as distinct from "somehow." There is no way, no method, no technique which you or I can use to come into accord with the Tao, the Way of Nature, because every how, every method implies a goal. And we cannot make the Tao a goal any more than we can aim an arrow at itself. If we once get into the tangled state of the arrow which is trying to shoot itself, the self trying to change itself, we can't do anything to stop it. So long as we think or feel that perhaps we can stop it, that there is some way, violent or subtle, difficult or easy, to make ourselves unselfish, the contradiction will continue or get worse. We have to see that there is no way. But in the state where we have realized that there is no way to be found, no result to be gained, the vicious circle breaks. *Ouroboros,* the snake eating his tail, has become conscious all the way round, and knows at last that that tail is the other end of his head.

We find ourselves in these circles because of ignorance, because of unconsciousness of the nature of our minds, of our thought-processes, of ourselves. And the antidote to ignorance is not action but knowledge—not what to do, but what we know. Yet here again, the necessary knowledge does not seem, on the surface, to be anything very promising or hopeful. For the only knowledge in this sphere which can be talked about is negative knowledge—knowledge of the trap, of our helpless imprisonment in useless seeking. Positive knowledge—of the Tao, of God, of the eternal Reality, is a matter of immediate, momentary experience. It can never be put into words, and any attempt to do so converts it into just another aspect of the trap. I realize that we do not like to be told that we are in a trap, and that there is nothing we can do to get out; still less do we like to realize it as a vivid experience. But there is no other way of release. A proverb says that man's extremity is God's opportunity. We cannot find release until we have known the real extremity of our situation, and see that all striving for spiritual ideals is completely futile— since the very seeking thrusts them away. Yet why should it surprise us? Hasn't it been said again and again that we must die to come to life, that heaven is always on the other side of the Valley of the Shadow of Death—the valley of which physical death is merely a symbol—where the helpless corpse, bound hand and foot in its winding sheet, is just a figure of the death in which we live so long as we mistake it for life? . . . Where do we go from here? We do not. *We* come to an end. But this is the end of the night.

# Lightness of Touch

CHESTERTON ONCE SAID THAT, BECAUSE THEY take themselves lightly, angels can fly. One sees so many faces dulled by a seriousness which, if it were born of grief, would be understandable. But the kind of seriousness which drags man down to the earth and kills the life of the spirit is not the child of sorrow but of a sort of playacting in which the player is deceived into identifying himself with his part. There is a seriousness in the play of children, but even this is different, for the child is aware that it is only playing and its seriousness is an indirect form of fun. But this seriousness becomes a vice in the adult, because he makes a religion of the game, so identifying himself with his part or position in life that he fears to lose it. This is especially so when the unenlightened man attains to any degree of responsibility; he develops a heaviness of touch, a lack of abandon, a stiffness which indicates that he is using his dignity as stilts to keep his head above adversity. His trouble is that instead of *playing* his part, his part plays him and makes him the laughingstock of all who see through his guise. The message of the Eastern wisdom is that the forms of life are *maya* and therefore profoundly lacking in seriousness from the viewpoint of reality. For the world of form and illusion which the majority take to be the real world is none other than the play of the Spirit, or, as the Hindus have called it, the Dance of Shiva. He is enlightened who joins in this play knowing it as play, for man suffers only because he takes seriously what the gods made for fun. Thus man only becomes man when he loses the gods' sense of levity. For the gods (or buddhas, or what you will) are simply our own innermost essence, and this could shatter the universe to nothingness in a moment if it willed. But it does not, and it keeps the worlds moving for the divine purpose of play, because, like a musician, it is a creator and delights in the fashioning of a rhythm and a melody. To play with it is therefore not a duty but a joy, and he who does not see it as a joy can neither do it nor understand it.

# Birds in the Sky

PASSING THROUGH THE SKY, AN ARROW OR A BIRD leaves no track. In Chinese and Indian philosophy, this is a recurrent metaphor which is used, strangely enough, for things which do not seem to resemble each other at all. The swift, trackless flight of the arrow is used as an image of impermanence, of the passage of human life through time, of the inevitable truth that all things must at last dissolve, and "leave not a track behind." Yet in one of the sayings of the Buddha, the invisible path of birds through the sky is likened to the way of life of a sage, to the superbly self-effacing kind of man of whom a Chinese poem says:

> Entering the forest, he does not disturb a blade of grass;
> Entering the water, he does not cause a ripple.

For the image represents a number of qualities which are, in fact, aspects of the same thing. It represents the sage's freedom and detachment of mind, a skylike consciousness in which experience moves without leaving any stain. As another poem says:

> The bamboo shadows sweep the stairs,
> But stir no dust.

Yet, paradoxically, this detachment *from* is also a harmony *with*, for the man who goes into the forest without disturbing a blade of grass is a man in no conflict with nature. Like the Native American scouts, he walks without a single twig cracking beneath his feet. Like the Japanese architects, he builds a house which seems to be a part of its natural surroundings. The image also represents the fact that the way of the sage cannot be traced and followed, since no authentic wisdom can be imitated. Each man must find it for himself, because there is really no way of putting it into words, of reaching it by any specific methods or directions.

But there is actually the most intimate connection between these two apparently separate uses of the metaphor—the way of the sage, on the one hand, and the impermanence of life, on the other. And the connection reveals the one deepest and most central principle of those Asian philosophies which so puzzle the Western mind by identifying the highest wisdom with what, to us, seems the doctrine of abject despair. Indeed, the word *despair* in a particular sense is the proper translation of the Hindu–Buddhist term *nirvana*—to "de-spirate," to breathe out, to give up the ghost. We cannot understand how the Asians manage to equate this despair with ultimate bliss—unless, as we are prone to suppose, they are after all a depraved and spineless people, long accustomed to fatalism and resignation.

I am constantly amazed at the way in which thoughtful Westerners—Christians in particular—seem almost *determined* to miss the point of this connection. For is not Christian imagery full of the theme of death as the essential prelude to eternal life? Is it not written that Christ himself "gave up the ghost," having cried out that he was forsaken by God? And is there not, in the Christian scriptures, a sufficient abundance of paradoxes about "having nothing, yet possessing all things," about finding the soul through losing it, and about the grain of corn that comes to fruition by its own death?

"Yes, indeed," say the clergymen, "*but* the Christian never *really* despairs, he never *really* dies. Through all tragedy, through all outward death and despair, he is fortified by an inward faith and hope that 'the best is yet to be.' He faces the worst that life can offer with the firm belief that ultimate reality is the God of love and justice, in whom is his hope for 'the life of the world to come.'"

Now, I think we say and feel and think so much about this hope that we miss the astounding eloquence of Buddhist *silence* upon the whole matter. So far as words, thoughts, ideas, and images are concerned, the doctrines of Buddhism and most forms of Hinduism are so negative and hopeless that they seem to be a sort of glorying in nihilism. They do not merely insist that human life is impermanent, that man has no immortal soul, and that in time every trace of our existence must vanish. They go on to indicate, as the wise man's goal, a release from this transient life which seems to be no release at all—a state called nirvana, which may be translated "despair," and the attainment of a metaphysical condition called *shunyata,* which is a voidness so void as to be neither existent nor nonexistent! For nonexistence *implies* existence as its logical correlate, whereas *shunyata* is so void that it does not imply anything at all.

Beyond this, if one can believe it possible, they go even a little further. Nirvana, which is already a negation enough in itself, is described in one text as no better than a dead stump to which to tie your donkey, and it is insisted that when you attain to it, you realize that no one has attained anything whatsoever. Perhaps I can put this in a more intelligible fashion. These doctrines first emphasize the somewhat grimly obvious fact that man has no abiding future. Without exception, everything that we attain or create, even the memorials that survive our death, must perish without trace, and that our quest for permanence is pure futility. Because, furthermore, happiness exists only in relation to misery, pleasure in relation to pain, the perceptive man does not try to separate them. The relation is so inseparable that, in some sense, happiness is misery, and pleasure is—because it implies—pain. Realizing this, he learns to abandon all desire for any happiness separate from misery, or pleasure apart from pain.

Naturally, however, this is hard to realize. I can, perhaps, understand verbally and intellectually that in desiring pleasure I am trying to quench my thirst with saltwater—since the more I get pleasure, the more I must want it. (And remember the old meaning of "want" as "lack"!) To want pleasure is to lack it. But still, I seem unable to be rid of the emotional habit of desiring it. If, then, I see that the desire for pleasure burns me by its implication of pain, I begin to desire not to desire, to desire nirvana, to seek to give up. In this, however, I have simply converted nirvana into another name for pleasure. For pleasure is by definition the object of desire. It is what we please, which is to say what we desire. If I discover that desire is suffering, and then desire not to desire, . . . well, I begin to get that "haven't-we-been-here-before?" feeling.

It is for this reason, then, that Buddhism suggests nirvana with terms that are negative and void, and not with the positive and desirable imagery which surrounds the notion of God. Nirvana is equated with *Shunyata,* the Nothing beyond nothing, to suggest that it is simply impossible to desire it. Whatever we are able to desire is still pleasure implying pain. Nirvana, release from suffering and desire, is called unattainable—not because it does not happen but because there is no way of seeking it.

Now the point of the emphasis upon impermanence is that every object of search, of desire, is in the end ungraspable and futile. To be delivered from futility, we must stop seeking. To seek for God, to desire God, is merely to drag Him down into the level of futile aims, or, in Christian language, to confuse the Creator with His creatures. Likewise, to desire nirvana is simply to make nirvana another name for ever-elusive pleasure. So long, then, as we think about God, talk about God, seek God, there is no God to be found.

Now, from the standpoint of Western culture, whether ancient or modern, Christian or secular, capitalist or communist, this is the great heresy. For Western culture is dedicated to the belief that there *is* a formula for happiness—an answer to the question "What shall I *do* to be saved?" All political propaganda, all advertising, and most of what we call education is based on the assumption that "there is a Way," and that it's only a matter of "know-how." (If some of the details haven't quite been worked out yet, just give the scientists a few more months and they'll have it.)

Well—when do we grow up? In a profession which combines philosophy, religion, psychology, and education, you meet so many people who have the answer, the great formula for human happiness—if only we could just put it into practice, which, for some reason or other we do not. Thus anyone who talks a lot about philosophy and psychology is supposed to be one of those who has the answers, and is more or less automatically cast in the social role of savior, preacher, counselor, and guide. The man who knows the way!

But there is no Way. Nobody knows the Way. The only way that there is is the path of a bird through the sky—now you see it, now you don't. Not a trace left. Life is not going anywhere; there is nothing to be attained. All striving and grasping is so much smoke in the clutch of a dissolving hand. We are all lost—kicked off into a void the moment we were born—and the only way is to fall into oblivion.

This *sounds* terrible. But this is because it is a half-truth. The other half cannot be put into words. It cannot be described, imagined, thought about. In words, this is the last word: everyone is dissolving into *nothing,* and no one can help it.

Is it possible, just for a moment, to realize this without jumping to conclusions, without crying *Pessimism, Despair,* or *Nihilism?* Is it too impossible to admit that all our well-laid traps for happiness are just so many ways of kidding ourselves that by meditation, psychoanalysis, Dianetics, Raja Yoga, Zen Buddhism, or mental science, *we* are somehow going to save ourselves from that final plop into nothing?

Because, if we do not see this much, then everything else in Asian philosophy, in Hinduism, Buddhism, Taoism, must remain a closed book. To know that you can do nothing is the beginning. Lesson One is: "I give up."

What happens now? You find yourself in what is perhaps a rather unfamiliar state of mind. Just watching. Not trying to get anything. Not expecting anything. Not hoping. Not seeking. Not trying to relax. Just watching, without purpose.

I should say nothing about what comes next. To hold out hope, to promise a result, spoils the whole thing. The final *word* must be, "There is no hope, no way." Yet there is no harm in just one more word—one more word about what lies on the other side of despair, provided we all understand that this something on the other side of despair cannot be hoped for, and is in any case thrust away by hoping.

The proverb says, "A watched pot never boils." We are all familiar with the many involuntary acts of the human body which never happen so long as we are trying to make them happen, so long as we are anxious about them—going to sleep, remembering a forgotten name, or, under certain circumstances, sexual excitation. Well, there is something like this which *happens* upon the sole condition that we are not trying to make it happen, that we have realized quite clearly that we *cannot* make it happen. In Zen, it is called satori, sudden awakening.

Perhaps we can see now the reason for the double meaning in the metaphor of the bird's path in the sky. Just as the bird leaves no trace, no record of its flight upon the void, so human desire can gain nothing out of life. But to realize this is at once to become the sage, since the greatest wisdom lies on the other side, immediately on the other side, of the greatest despair. It is, of course, something more than despair—a joy, a sense of creative life and power, I might even say a security and certainty, beyond any imagining. But this is a way of feeling which the will and the imagination are as unable to bring about as to make one's bones grow or decrease the speed of the pulse. They must happen by themselves.

In the same way, all that is positive, the whole creative content, of that spiritual experience which is called awakening, nirvana, must of necessity happen by itself. It not only cannot but *must* not be induced by trying and willing, since anything that one could will wouldn't be *it*.

# Walking on the Wheel

ALMOST EVERY FUNDAMENTAL PRINCIPLE OF LIFE can be expressed in two opposite ways. There are those who say that to attain the highest wisdom we must be still and calm, immovable in the midst of turmoil. And there are those who say that we must move on as life moves, never stopping for a moment either in fear of what is to come or to turn a regretful glance at what has gone. The former are as those who listen to music, letting the flow of notes pass through their minds without trying either to arrest them or to speed them on. Like Chuang-tzu's perfect man, they employ their minds as a mirror: it grasps nothing; it refuses nothing; it receives, but does not keep. The latter are as those who dance to music, keeping pace with its movement and letting their limbs flow with it as unceasingly and as unhesitatingly as clouds respond to the breath of wind. The one seems to reflect events as they pass, and the other to move forward with them. Both points of view, however, are true, for to attain that highest wisdom we must at once walk on and remain still. Consider life as a revolving wheel set upright with man walking on its tire. As he walks, the wheel is revolving toward him beneath his feet, and if he is not to be carried backward by it and flung to the ground he must walk at the same speed as the wheel turns. If he exceeds that speed, he will topple forward and slip off the wheel onto his face. For at every moment we stand, as it were, on the top of a wheel; immediately we try to cling to that moment, to that particular point of the wheel, it is no longer at the top and we are off our balance. Thus by not trying to seize the moment, we keep it, for the second we fail to walk on we cease to remain still. Yet within this there is a still deeper truth. From the standpoint of eternity we never can and never do leave the top of the wheel, for if a circle is set in infinite space it has neither top nor bottom. Wherever you stand is the top, and it revolves only because you are pushing it round with your own feet.

# The Language of
# Metaphysical Experience

THERE IS AN AREA OF HUMAN EXPERIENCE FOR
which we do not have any really suitable name in our Western
languages, for while it is basic to such matters as religion, metaphysics, and mysticism, it is not identical with any one of them.
I refer to the perennial type of experience which is described as a
more or less immediate knowledge of God, or of the ultimate
reality, ground, or essence of the universe, by whatever name it
may be represented.*

According to the ancient spiritual traditions of both Europe
and Asia, which include ways of life and thought as widely different as Buddhism and Catholicism, this experience is the supreme
fulfillment of human life—the goal, the final end, toward which
human existence is ordered.

According, however, to modern logical philosophy—scientific
empiricism, logical positivism, and the like—statements of this
kind are simply meaningless. While it is admitted that there may
be interesting and delightful experiences of the "mystical" type,
logical philosophy finds it altogether illegitimate to regard them

*I have not simply equated this experience with "mysticism" since the latter
frequently contains symbolic and affective elements which are by no means
essential to the order of experience I am discussing.

as containing any knowledge of a metaphysical character, as constituting an experience of "ultimate reality" or the Absolute.

This critique is based not so much upon a psychological analysis of the experience itself as upon purely logical analysis of such universal concepts as God, Ultimate Reality, Absolute Being, and the like—all of which are shown to be terms without meaning. It is not the purpose of this paper to describe the steps of this critique in any detail, since it should be familiar enough to every student of modern philosophy, and since there seems no need to take issue with the logical argument itself. The starting point of this paper is one which—perversely, it may seem—regards the basic argument of modern logical philosophy as a highly important contribution to metaphysical thought—enabling us to evaluate the true character and function of metaphysical terms and symbols far less confusedly than has hitherto been possible.

This evaluation, however, is not the sort of devaluation which the individual exponents of logical philosophy, such as Russell, Ayer, and Reichenbach, propose. For the positive contribution of logical philosophy to metaphysics and religion has been obscured by the fact that such exponents were not content to be logicians. Because of a certain emotional bias against religious or metaphysical points of view, this logical critique has been used as an instrument in a polemic, even a propaganda, with emotional rather than logical motivations.

It is one thing to demonstrate that the concept of Being is without logical meaning. It is quite another to go on to say that this, and similar metaphysical concepts, are not philosophy but poetry, where the term "poetry" carries a very strongly implied "pooh-pooh." The implication is that the "poetry" of religious and metaphysical symbols may be cause or effect of very exquisite and inspiring emotional experiences, but these, like "the arts" in wartime, are among the nonessentials of life. The serious philosopher regards them as charming toys—as means of decorating life, not of understanding it—in somewhat the same way as a physician might adorn his office with a medicine mask from the South Seas. All this is merely damning with faint praise.

While the exponents of logical philosophy have, on their side, sought to devalue the insights of metaphysics and religion, the would-be defenders of Faith have for the most part looked around somewhat ineffectually for means of defeating logical philosophy at its own game. On the whole, the more successful counterattack has seemed to be returning one pooh-pooh for another; as, for instance, the quip that Ayer, Reichenbach, and company have exchanged philosophy for grammar.

Yet in the context of Western philosophy and religion this situation is not at all surprising, for we have always been under the impression that religio-metaphysical statements are of the same order as scientific and historical statements. We have generally taken it for granted that the proposition "there is a God" is a statement of the same kind as "there are stars in the sky." The assertion that "all things have being" has always seemed to convey information in the same way as the assertion that "all men are mortal." Furthermore, "the universe was made by God" has seemed as much a statement of the historical type as that "the telephone was invented by Alexander Graham Bell."

Dr. F.S.C. Northrop is thus perfectly correct in pointing to the essential similarity between science, on the one hand, and the Hebrew–Christian religious tradition, on the other, insofar as both are concerned with "truth" as a structure of objective reality, whose nature is determinate even if unseen. Indeed, the scientific spirit has its historical origins in the type of mentality which is concerned to know the supernatural and the unseen in terms of positive propositions, which wants to know *what facts* lie beneath the surface of events. Thus Christian theology and science stand in somewhat the same historical relation as astrology and astronomy, alchemy and chemistry, both constituting a body of theory to explain the past and predict the future.*

But Christianity did not disappear with the alchemists. Since the rise of modern science, theology has played a most problematic role. It has taken many different attitudes to science, ranging from denouncing it as a rival doctrine, through conciliation and adaptation, to a sort of withdrawal in which it is felt that theology speaks of a realm of being inaccessible to scientific inquiry. Throughout, there has been the general assumption on the part of both theologians and scientists that the two disciplines were employing the same kind of language, and were interested in the same order of objective, determinate truths. Indeed, when some theologians speak of God as having "an objective, supernatural reality, independent of our minds and of the sensible world," it is impossible to see how their language differs from that of science. For it appears that God is some specific thing or fact—an objective existence—supernatural in the sense that He or It is imperceptible within the "wave band" of our sense-organs and scientific instruments.

Where this confusion between the nature of religious or metaphysical statements, on the one hand, and scientific or historical statements, on the other, remains unclarified, it will, of course, be difficult indeed to see how modern logical philosophy can make any positive contribution to metaphysics. In a theological system where God plays the part of a scientific hypothesis, that is, a means of explaining and predicting the course of events, it is easy enough to show that the hypothesis adds nothing to our knowledge. One does not explain what happens by saying that

---

*Of course, there are other interpretations of the proper functions of alchemy and astrology, representing their aims as utterly different from those of science. Deeply understood, neither alchemy nor astrology have to do with the prediction and control of *future* events, but are rather a symbolism of *eternal* "events" and the process of their realization in the *present*.

God wills it. For if everything that happens is by divine intention or permission, the will of God becomes merely another name for "everything that happens." Upon logical analysis, the statement, "Everything is the will of God," turns out to be the tautology, "Everything is everything."

To cut a long story short, thus far the contribution of logical philosophy to metaphysics has been entirely negative. The verdict seems to be that, under logical scrutiny, the entire body of metaphysical doctrine consists either of tautology or nonsense. But this amounts to a total "debunking" of metaphysics only as it has been understood in the West—as consisting of meaningful statements conveying information about "transcendental objects." Asian philosophy has never been of the serious opinion that metaphysical statements convey information of a positive character. Their function is not to denote "Reality" as an object of knowledge, but to "cure" a psychological process by which man frustrates and tortures himself with all kinds of unreal problems. To the Asian mind, "Reality" cannot be expressed; it can only be known intuitively by getting rid of unreality, of contradictory and absurd ways of thinking and feeling.

The primary contribution of logical philosophy in this sphere is simply the confirmation of a point which has long been clear to both Hindus and Buddhists, though perhaps less widely realized in the Christian tradition. The point is that the attempt to talk about, think about, or know about ultimate Reality constitutes an impossible task. If epistemology is the attempt to know what knows, and ontology the attempt to define "is-ness," they are clearly circular and futile procedures, like trying to bite one's own teeth. In a commentary on the Kena Upanishad, Shankara says:

> Now a distinct and definite knowledge is possible in respect of everything capable of becoming an object of knowledge:

but it is not possible in the case of That which cannot become such an object. That is Brahman, for It is the Knower, and the Knower can know other things, but cannot make Itself the object of Its own knowledge, in the same way that fire can burn other things but cannot burn itself.

In the same way, the Brihadaranyaka Upanishad says:

Thou couldst not see the seer of sight, thou couldst not hear the hearer of hearing, nor perceive the perceiver of perception, now know the knower of knowledge. (iii, 4. 2)

Or in the words of a Chinese Buddhist poem:

It is like a sword that wounds, but cannot wound itself;
Like an eye that sees, but cannot see itself.*

A similar difficulty exists for physics in any attempt to investigate the nature of energy. For there is a point at which physics, as much as metaphysics, enters the realm of tautology and nonsense because of the circular character of the task which it attempts—to study electrons with instruments which are, after all, electrons themselves. At the risk of quoting a source which is somewhat passé, the classical statement of this problem is in Eddington's *Nature of the Physical World:*

We have perhaps forgotten that there was a time when we wanted to be told what an electron is. The question was never answered. . . . *Something unknown is doing we don't know what*—that is what our theory amounts to. It does

*Zenrin Kushu*—an anthology of Chinese poetry employed in the study and practice of Zen Buddhism.

44

not sound a particularly illuminating theory. I have read something like it elsewhere:

> The slithy toves
> Did gyre and gimble in the wabe.

There is the same suggestion of activity. There is the same indefiniteness as to the nature of the activity and of what it is that is acting.*

Eddington goes on to point out that, despite this indefiniteness, physics can "get results" because the electrons, the unknowns within the atom, are countable.

Eight slithy toves gyre and gimble in the oxygen wabe; seven in nitrogen. By admitting a few numbers, even "Jabberwocky" may become scientific. We can now venture on a prediction: if one of its toves escapes, oxygen will be masquerading in garb properly belonging to nitrogen. . . . It would not be a bad reminder of the essential unknownness of the fundamental entities of physics to translate it into "Jabberwocky"; provided all numbers—all metrical attributes—are unchanged, it does not suffer in the least.†

The point which emerges is that what we are counting or measuring in physics, and that what we are experiencing in everyday life as sense data, is at root unknown and probably unknowable.

At this point, modern logical philosophy dismisses the problem and turns its attention to something else on the assumption that the unknowable need not and cannot concern us further. It asserts that questions which have neither the physical nor the logical possibility of an answer are not real questions. But this

---

*Eddington, Sir Arthur Stanley. *Nature of the Physical World* (London, 1935), 280.
†*Ibid.*, 281.

assertion does not get rid of the common human *feeling* that such unknowns or unknowables as electrons, energy, existence, consciousness, or "Reality" are in some way *queer*. The very fact of not being able to know them makes them all the stranger. Only a rather dry kind of mind turns away from them—a mind interested in nothing but logical structures. The more complete kind of mind, which can feel as well as think, remains to "indulge" the odd sense of mystery which comes from contemplating the fact that everything is at base something which cannot be known. Every statement which you make about this "something" turns out to be nonsense. And what is specially strange is that this unknowable something is also the basis of that which otherwise I know so intimately—myself.

Western man has a peculiar passion for order and logic, such that, for him, the entire significance of life consists in putting experience into order. What is ordered is predictable, and thus a basis for "safe bets." We tend to show a psychological resistance to areas of life and experience where logic, definition, and order—that is, "knowledge" in our sense—are inapplicable. For this type of mind the realm of indeterminacy and Brownian movements is frankly embarrassing, and the contemplation of the fact that everything is reducible to something we cannot think about is even disquieting. There is no real "reason" why it should be disquieting, because our inability to know what electrons are does not seem to interfere with our capacity to predict their behavior in our own macroscopic world.

The resistance is not based on some fear of an unpredictable action which the unknown may produce, although I suspect that even the most hardened logical positivist would have to admit to some odd feelings in face of an unknown called death. The resistance is rather the fundamental unwillingness of this type of mind to contemplate the limits of its power to succeed, order, and control. It feels that if there are areas of life which it cannot order, it is surely reasonable (i.e., orderly) to forget them and turn to areas of life which *can* be ordered—so that the sense of success, of the mind's own competence, can be maintained. The contemplation of these intellectual limitations is, for the pure intellectual, a humiliation. But for the man who is something more than a calculator, the baffling is also the wonderful. In the face of the unknowable he feels with Goethe that

> the highest to which man can attain is wonder; and if the prime phenomenon makes him wonder, let him be content; nothing higher can it give him, and nothing further should he seek for behind it; here is the limit.

In the type of metaphysical or mystical experience which we are discussing, this feeling of wonder—which has all kinds of depths and subtleties—is one of two major components. The other is a feeling of liberation (the Hindu *Moksha*) which attends the realization that an immense amount of human activity is directed to the solution of unreal and purely fantastic problems—to the attainment of goals which we do not actually desire.

*Speculative* metaphysics—ontology and epistemology—are the intellectual aspects of fantastic problems which are basically psychological, and by no means confined to persons of a philosophical or even religious turn of mind. As already indicated, the essential nature of this kind of problem is circular—the attempt to know the knower, to make fire burn fire. This is why Buddhism speaks of release, nirvana, as deliverance from the Wheel, and of seeking Reality as "like looking for an ox when you are riding on one."

The psychological basis of these circular problems becomes clear when we look into the assumptions upon which, for example, the problems of ontology are based. What premises of thought and feeling underlie men's efforts to know "being," "existence," or "energy" as objects? Clearly, one assumption is that these names refer to objects—an assumption which could not have been made if there were not beneath it the further assumption that "I," the knowing subject, am somehow different from "being," the supposed object. If it were perfectly clear that the question, "What is being?" is, in the final analysis, the same question as "What am I?," the circular and futile character of the question would have been obvious from the beginning. But that it was far from clear is shown by the fact that metaphysical epistemology could ask the question, "What am I?" or "What is that which is conscious?" without recognizing a still more obvious circle. Obviously, questions of this order could be taken seriously only because of some nonlogical feeling of the need for an answer.

This feeling—common, perhaps, to most human beings—is surely the sense that "I," the subject, am a unique, isolated entity. There would be no need whatsoever to wonder *what* I am unless in some way I felt strange to myself. But so long as my consciousness feels strange to, cut off, and separate from its own roots, I can *feel* meaning in an epistemological question which has no logical sense. For I feel that consciousness is a function of "I"— not recognizing that "I," the ego, is just another name for consciousness. The statement "I am conscious" is, then, a concealed tautology saying only that consciousness is a function of consciousness. It can escape from this circularity upon the sole condition that "I" is taken to mean very much more than consciousness or its contents. But, in the West, this is not a usual use of the word. We identify "I" with the conscious will, and do not admit moral authority or responsibility for what we do unconsciously and unintentionally—the implication being that such acts are not our deeds but merely events which "happen" within us. When "I" is identified with "consciousness," man feels himself to be a detached, separate, and uprooted entity acting "freely" in a void.

This uprooted feeling is doubtless responsible for the psychological insecurity of Western man, and his passion for imposing the values of order and logic upon the whole of his experience. Yet while it is obviously absurd to say that consciousness is a function of consciousness, there seems to be no means of knowing that of which consciousness *is* a function. That which knows—and which psychologists call somewhat paradoxically the unconscious—is never the object of its own knowledge.

Now, consciousness, the ego, feels uprooted so long as it avoids and refuses to accept the fact that it does not and cannot know its own base or ground. But when this is recognized, the consciousness *feels* connected, rooted, even though it does not know *to what* it is connected, *in what* it is rooted. So long as it retains delusions of self-sufficiency, omni-competence, and individual free will, it ignores the unknown on which it rests. By the familiar "law of reversed effort," this refusal of the unknown brings the feeling of insecurity, and in its train all the frustrating and impossible problems, all the vicious circles of human life, from the exalted nonsense of ontology down to the vulgar realms of power politics, where individuals play at being God. The hideous contrivances of the police (the 100 percent safe and ordered) state for planning the planners and guarding the guards and investigating the investigators are simply the political and social equivalents of the quests of speculative metaphysics. Both alike have their psychological origin in the reluctance of consciousness, of the ego, to face its own limits, and to admit that the ground and essence of the known is the unknown.

It does not matter very much whether you call this unknown Brahman or Blah, though the latter term usually indicates the intention to forget it, and the former to keep it in mind. Keeping it in mind, the law of reversed effort works in the other direction.

I realize that my very substance, that which I am, is altogether beyond grasping or knowing. It is not "I"—a word which suggests that it means something, it is non-sense and no-thing, which is why Mahayana Buddhism calls it *Tathata,* of which a good translation might be "da-da," and *shunyata,* the "void" or indeterminate. Similarly, the Vedantins say, *"Tat tvam asi"*— *"That* are thou"—without ever giving a positive designation of what *that* is. The man who tries to know, to grasp himself, becomes insecure, just as one suffocates by holding one's breath. Conversely, the man who really knows that he cannot grasp himself gives up, relaxes, and is at ease. But he never really knows if he simply dismisses the problem, and does not pause to wonder, to feel, and to become vividly aware of the real impossibility of self-knowledge.

To the religious mentality of the modern West, this entirely negative approach to Reality is almost incomprehensible, for it suggests only that the world is based on the shifting sands of nonsense and caprice. For those who equate sanity with order this is a doctrine of pure despair. Yet little more than five hundred years ago a Catholic mystic was saying of God, "By love He may be gotten and holden, but by thought never," and that God must be known through "unknowing," through "mystical ignorance."* And the love of which he spoke was not emotion. It was the general state of mind which exists when a man, through the realization of its impossibility, is no longer trying to grasp himself, to order everything and be dictator of the universe.

In our own day, logical philosophy provides the same tech-

*Dom Justin McCann, ed., *The Cloud of Unknowing* (London, 1943). The doctrine of "knowing God by unknowing (*agnosia*)" derives from the sixth-century Syrian metaphysician writing under the name of Dionysius the Areopagite, and in particular from his *Theologia Mystica,* in Migne's *Patrologia Graeca,* vol. 3. A translation of the latter work is included in Father McCann's edition of the former.

nique of negation, telling us that in every statement in which we think we have grasped or defined or merely designated Reality, we have uttered only nonsense. When the tongue tries to put *itself* into words, the most that may be expected is a tongue twister. For this reason, the procedures of logical philosophy will only be disquieting to those theologians and metaphysicians who imagine that their definitions of the Absolute actually define anything. But it was always perfectly clear to the philosophers of Hinduism and Buddhism, and to some fewer Catholic mystics, that words such as "Brahman," "Tathata," and "God" meant not something but no-thing. They indicated a void in knowledge, somewhat as a window is outlined by the frame.

Yet logical philosophy pursues its criticism further, and says that nonsense statements and exclamations of this order do not constitute philosophy because they contribute nothing to knowledge—by which they mean that they do not assist us to predict anything, and offer no directions for human conduct. That is, in part, true, though it misses the very obvious point that philosophy—wisdom—consists as much in its spaces as in its lines, in recognizing what is not and cannot be known as in the contrary. But we must go farther than this truism. Knowledge is more than know-how, and wisdom is more than predicting and ordering. Human life becomes a fantastic vicious circle when man tries to order and control the world and himself beyond certain limits, and these "negative metaphysics" at least convey the positive injunction to relax this excess of effort.

But beyond this they have a positive consequence which is still more important. They "integrate" logic and conscious thought with the indeterminate matrix, the nonsense, which we find at the root of all things. The assumption that the task of philosophy, as of human life, is fulfilled only in predicting and ordering, and that the "nonsensical" has no value, rests upon a sort of philosophical "schizophrenia." If man's work is entirely to go to war on chaos with logic, to determine the indeterminate; if the "good" is the logical and the "evil" the whimsical; then logic, consciousness, and the human brain is in conflict with the source of its own life and ability. We must never forget that the processes which form this brain are unconscious, and that beneath all the perceptible orders of the macroscopic world lies the indeterminate nonsense of the microscopic, the "gyring" and "gimbling" of a "tove" called energy—about which we know nothing. *Ex nihilo omnia fiunt.* But this nothing is a very strange thing.

Logical philosophy does not seem to have faced the fact that "nonsense" terms, so far from being valueless, are essential to every system of thought. It would be quite impossible to construct a philosophy or a science which is a "closed system" rigorously defining every term which it employs. Gödel has given us a clear mathematicological proof of the fact that no system can define its own axioms without self-contradiction, and, since Hilbert, modern mathematics employs the point as an entirely undefined concept. Just as the knife cuts other things, but not itself, so thought uses tools which define but cannot be defined; logical philosophy itself by no means escapes from this limitation.

For example, when logical philosophy asserts that "true meaning is a verifiable hypothesis," it must recognize that this very statement is meaningless if unverifiable. Similarly, when it insists that the only realities are those "facts" which are elicited in "scientific observation," it must recognize that it cannot, and does not, answer the question "What is a fact?" If we say that "facts" or "things" are the segments of experience symbolized by nouns, we are merely shifting the irreducible element of nonsense in our definition from "fact" to "experience." Some basic nonsense is entirely unavoidable, and the attempt to construct a completely self-defining system of thought is a vicious circle of tautology. Language can hardly dispense with the word "is," and yet the dictionary can only inform us that "what is" is "what exists," and that "what exists" is "what is."

If, then, it must be admitted that even one nonsense, meaningless, or undefined term is necessary to all thought, we have already admitted the metaphysical principle that the basis or ground of all "things" is an indefinable (or infinite) nothing beyond sense—always escaping our comprehension and control. This is the supernatural, in the proper sense of what cannot be "natured" or classified, and the immaterial in the sense of what cannot be measured, metered, or "mattered." In all its fullness, this admission is precisely *faith*—the recognition that one must ultimately "give in" to a life-source, a Self beyond the ego, which lies beyond the definition of thought and the control of action.

Belief, in the *popular* Christian sense, falls short of this faith, since its object is a God conceived as having a determinate nature. But to the extent that God can be a known object of definite nature, He is an idol, and belief in such a God is idolatry. Thus in the very act of demolishing the concept of the Absolute as a "what" or "fact" about which meaningful statements and determinations can be made, logical philosophy has made its most vital contribution to religious faith—at the cost of its antithesis, religious "belief." While the logical positivists unwittingly join forces with the Hebrew prophets in their denunciation of idolatry, the prophets are found to be in line with that grand metaphysical tradition which, in Hinduism and Buddhism, has taken the disuse of idols to its proper conclusion.

In sum, then, the function of metaphysical "statements" in Hinduism and Buddhism is neither to convey positive information about an Absolute, nor to indicate an experience in which this Absolute becomes an object of knowledge. In the words of the Kena Upanishad: "Brahman is unknown to those who know It, and is known to those who do not know It at all." This knowing of Reality by unknowing is the psychological state of the man whose ego is no longer split or dissociated from its experiences, who no longer feels himself as an isolated embodiment of logic and consciousness, separate from the "gyring" and "gimbling" of the unknown. He is thus delivered from *samsara,* the Wheel, the squirrel cage psychology of all those human beings who everlastingly frustrate themselves with impossible tasks of knowing the knower, controlling the controller, and organizing the organizer, like *ouroboros,* the mixed-up snake, who dines off his own tail.

# Good Intentions

IT IS AN OLD SAYING THAT THE ROAD TO HELL IS paved with good intentions. Those who believe that motive is the most important factor in any undertaking will be puzzled by this saying. For is not Right Motive the first step in the Buddha's Path, and is it not stressed again and again that each step is set about with danger if the motive for taking it is not pure? But beware of good motives. There are good intentions and good intentions, and things are not always what they seem. Nothing is easier than to give up the world because one is incompetent in the affairs of the world. There is no wisdom in scorning riches simply because one is unable to obtain them, nor in despising the pleasures of the senses because one has not the means of fulfilling them. If the desire for these things exists, and if that desire is thwarted by circumstance, to add self-deception to frustration is to exchange a lesser hell for a greater. No hell is worse than that in which one lives without knowing it.

For the desire which is scorned for no other reason than that it cannot be satisfied is the greatest of man's enemies. One may pretend that it does not exist, that one has surrendered it, but one must sincerely answer the question, "If I *could* satisfy that desire, would I?" If that is not answered, to make a show of giving up the world, to take up the ascetic life not of desire but of necessity and to pride oneself upon it, that is to hide one's face from the enemy and so become doubly vulnerable. Thus the first step on the Path is to know *what* you want, not what you *ought* to want. Only in this way can the pilgrim set out upon his journey fully prepared. Otherwise he is like a general that leads a campaign into an unknown territory, who, instead of ascertaining his own strength and the strength and position of his foe, concerns himself only with what he imagines these things *ought* to be. And however good his imaginations, he will without doubt lead his army into a hell.

# Zen

ALTHOUGH ZEN IS A WORD OF ONLY THREE LET-
ters, three volumes would not explain it, nor even three libraries
of volumes. If one were to compile books on the subject to the
end of time, they would not explain it, for all that could be written would only be ideas *about* Zen, not Zen itself. Indeed, who-
ever imagines he has explained Zen has in fact only explained it
away; it can no more be bound by a definition than the wind can
be shut in a box without ceasing to be wind. Thus any attempt to
write on Zen may seem an absurdity from the beginning, but that
is only so if either reader or writer imagines that Zen can be
contained in a set of ideas. A book about London is in no sense
London itself, and no sane person would dream of thinking that
it is. Yet apparently intelligent people often make the equally ridiculous mistake of identifying a philosophical system, a dogma,
a creed, with Ultimate Truth, imagining that they have found
that Truth embraced in a set of propositions which appeals to
their reason. There are thousands of men and women searching
through volume after volume, visiting religious societies, and at-
tending the lectures of famous teachers in the vain hope that they
will one day come upon some explanation of the mysteries of life:
some saying, some idea, which will contain the solution to the
Infinite Riddle. Some continue the search till they die, others
imagine that in various ideologies they have found what they

desire, and a few penetrate beyond ideas about Truth to Truth itself. There are some religions and philosophies which lend themselves more easily than others to the error of mistaking the idea for the reality, religions in which the creed and the symbol are emphasized at the expense of the spiritual experience which they are intended to embody. This, however, is less a reflection on those religions than on the ignorance of their devotees. But there is at least one cult in which this error is almost impossible, precisely because it has no creed, no philosophical system, no canon of scriptures, no intellectually comprehensible doctrine. So far as it can be called a definite cult at all, it consists of devices for freeing the soul from its fetters, devices which are picturesquely described as fingers pointing at the moon—and he is a fool who mistakes the finger for the moon. This cult is Zen, a form of Buddhism that developed in China and now flourishes principally in Japan. Zen is itself a Japanese word, derived from the Chinese *Ch'an* or *Ch'an-na*, a form of the Sanskrit *dhyana*, which is usually rendered in English as "meditation" or "contemplation." This, however, is a misleading translation, for although in the terminology of yoga *dhyana* signifies a certain state of contemplation, a state of what we should somewhat inaccurately call "trance," *Zen* is a far more inclusive term. We come nearer to its meaning if we remember that the word *dhyana* is related to *gñana* (the Greek *gnosis)* or Knowledge in the very highest sense of that word, which is to say supreme spiritual enlightenment. *Gñana* (another form of which is sometimes spelled *dzyan)* is very close to Zen, the more so when we remember that Zen is said to have come into the world at the moment when Gautama the Buddha found Enlightenment when sitting one night under the famous Bodhi Tree at Bodh-gaya in northern India. There, according to the teachers of Zen, he found something which cannot be expressed in any form of words; an experience which every man must undergo for himself; which can no more be passed on from one man to another than you can eat another person's food for him.

Zen, however, as a specific cult, is mainly a product of the Chinese mind. Buddhism developed in India as a highly subtle and abstract system of philosophy, a cult of sublime other-worldliness perfectly suited to the inhabitants of a hot climate where life is able to flourish with little labour. The Chinese and Japanese, on the other hand, have a climate nearer to our own and have the same practical bent as the peoples of northern Europe. Perhaps the greatest triumph of Buddhism is that it was able to adapt itself to a mentality so far removed from the Indian. Thus Zen has been described as the Chinese revolt against Buddhism. It would be nearer the truth to call it the Chinese interpretation of Buddhism, although the term "revolt" certainly conveys the fierce, almost iconoclastic character of Zen—a cult which has no patience with any practice or formula which has not immediate relationship with the one thing of importance: Enlightenment. To understand this revolt or interpretation (or better, "revolutionary interpretation") some of the fundamental principles of Buddhism must be borne in mind.

The Buddha, who lived some 600 years BCE, taught that life, as we live it, is necessarily unharmonious because of the selfish, possessive attitude we adopt towards it. In Sanskrit this attitude is called *trishna* (often mistranslated "desire"), and though there is no one word for it in English, it may be understood as the craving to resist change, to "save our own skins" at all costs, to possess those whom we love; in fact, to hold on to life "like grim death." And that particular phrase has its moral. If anything that lives and moves is held, it dies just like a plucked flower. Egotism is a fierce holding on to oneself; it is building oneself up in a haughty stronghold, refusing to join in the play of life, refusing to accept the eternal laws of change of movement to which all are subject. But that refusal can only be illusion. Whether we like it or not, change comes, and the greater the resistance, the greater the pain. Buddhism perceives the beauty of change, for life is like music in this: if any note or phrase is held for longer than its appointed time, the melody is lost. Thus Buddhism may be summed up in two phrases: "Let go!" and "Walk on!" Drop the craving for self, for permanence, for particular circumstances, and go straight ahead with the movement of life. The state of mind thereby attained is called Nirvana. But this is a teaching easy to misunderstand, for it is so easy to represent the doctrine of "letting go" as an utter denial of life and the world, and Nirvana as a state infinitely removed from all earthly concerns.

Zen, however, corrected this error in the most surprising and unique manner—so much so that a great part of the Zen teachings may appear at first to be mere buffoonery or nonsense.

A disciple came to Zen Master Chao-chou and asked, "I have just come to this monastery. Would you mind giving me some instruction, please?"

The master replied, "Have you eaten your breakfast yet, or not?"

"Yes, I have, sir."

"Then wash your dishes."

It is said that as a result of this remark the disciple was suddenly enlightened as to the whole meaning of Zen.

On another occasion a master was about to address an assembly of students when a bird began to sing in a nearby tree. The master remained silent until the bird had finished, and then, announcing that his address had been given, went away.

Another master set a pitcher before two of his disciples. "Do not call it a pitcher," he said, "but tell me what it is." One replied, "It cannot be called a piece of wood." The master, however, was not satisfied with this answer, and he turned to the other disciple who simply knocked the pitcher over and walked away.

This action had the master's full approval. It will be asked whether these antics have the least connection with religion, even with ordinary sanity. They are regarded by the exponents of Zen as full of the deepest significance, and when we remember that Zen has been, beyond question, one of the most powerful influences in shaping the art and culture of the Far East, such behavior is entitled to respect. Has it some symbolic meaning? What is it about? The answer is that it has no symbolic meaning, and that it is *about* nothing. But it is something, and that something is that very obvious but much ignored thing—*life*. The Zen master is in fact demonstrating life in its actuality; without words or ideas he is teaching his disciples to know life directly. Sometimes in answer to a religious question he will give a smack on the face, returning a reality for an abstraction. If he gave a reasoned answer, the disciple would be able to analyze it, to subject it to intellectual dissection, and to imagine a mere lifeless formula as a living truth. But with a smack, a bird, a pitcher, a heap of dishes there can be no mistake. A smack is here one moment and gone the next. There is nothing you can catch hold of, nothing other than a most lively fact, as much alive as the passing moment which can never be made to stay. And a bird is a bird; you hear its song, but you cannot seize the notes to make them continue.

It just is, and is gone, and you feel the beauty of its song precisely because the notes do not wait for you to analyze them. Therefore the Zen master is not trying to give you ideas *about* life; he is trying to give you life itself, to make you realize life in and around you, to make you live it instead of being a mere spectator, a mere pedant absorbed in the dry bones of something which the life has long deserted. A symphony is not explained by a mathematical analysis of its notes; the mystery of a woman's beauty is not revealed by a postmortem dissection; and no one ever understood the wonder of a bird on the wing by stuffing it and putting it in a glass case. To understand these things, you must live and move with them as they are alive. The same is true of the universe: no amount of intellectual analysis will explain it, for philosophy and science can only reveal its mechanism, never its meaning or, as the Chinese say, its Tao.

"What is the Tao?" A Zen master answers, "Usual life is the very Tao."

"How does one bring oneself into accord with it?" "If you try to accord with it, you will get away from it."

For to imagine that there is a "you" separate from life which somehow has to accord with life is to fall straight into the trap. If you try to find the Tao, you are at once presupposing a difference between yourself and the Tao. Therefore the Zen masters say nothing about the means for becoming Enlightened, for understanding the Tao. They simply concentrate on Tao itself. When you are reading a book you defeat your purpose altogether if you think about yourself trying to concentrate on it; instead of thinking about what is written, your attention is absorbed in your efforts to concentrate. The secret is to think of the book and forget yourself. But that is not all. The book is of little use to you if you go to the other extreme and simply let it "run away with you." On the contrary, you must bring your own understanding and intelligence to it, and then through the union of your own thoughts and the thoughts in the book, something new is born. This union is the important task; you must just do it, and not waste energy in thinking about doing it. The same is true in Zen. It does not ask that we should so submit ourselves to life that the world altogether masters us and blots us out. There are some who never live, who are always having thoughts about life and feelings about life; others are swept away on the tides of circumstance, so overwhelmed by events that they have nothing of their own.

Buddhism, however, is the Middle Way, and this is not a compromise but a union between opposites to produce a "higher third"; just as man and woman unite to produce a child. The same process is found in almost every religion, in some deeply hidden, in others plainly revealed. In Christianity man must be born anew of water and the spirit, symbols of substance and energy, concrete life and the mind of man. Thus the prayer to Christ to be "born in us" is the hope for the same Enlightenment that we find in Buddhism and the story of Christ's birth is its allegory. For the Holy Ghost is spirit, and Mary (from the Latin word *mare*—sea, water) is the world, called in Sanskrit *maya*. And the mother of the Buddha was also called Maya, and he too was supposed to have been miraculously conceived. Thus the realization of the Christ within, the Buddha within, the Tao within, or the Krishna within is in each instance the result of a process which Zen presents to us in this unique and almost startling manner. It is the understanding of the One which lies behind the Many; the bringing together of opposites, of subject and object, the ego and the universe, to create the Holy Child.

And yet we must beware of that definition, of that convenient summary of religious endeavor. It so easily becomes a mere catchphrase, a truth so fastened in a nutshell that it ceases to be of the least use. In its prison it withers away and dies. Therefore Zen comes at this stage with a most inconvenient question, "When the Many are reduced to the One, to what is the One to be reduced?" Only he who knows what that is understands Zen. It would be futile to try to explain any further, for to do so would be to defeat the very purpose of Zen, which is to make everyone find out for himself. It is like a detective story with the last chapter missing; it remains a mystery, a thing like a beam of light which can be seen and used, but never caught—loved, but never possessed. And by that we may know that Zen is life.

# The One

THE DOCTRINES OF RELIGION ARE SYMBOLS USED by saints and sages to describe spiritual experiences, just as ordinary men use words to describe mental and physical experiences. Students of religion recognize two kinds of spiritual experience, of which the first resembles what we call a state of mind, such as happiness, love, or fear; and the second an experience of something outside ourselves, as when we see stars, trees, or hills. In the language of religion, the first kind of experience may be called the sense of freedom, salvation, or deliverance, and the second a beatific vision. The doctrines of religion have their origin in attempts to convey these experiences to others by enshrining a state of mind within an idea about the universe or by recording a vision as the basis of an article of faith. Visions are somewhat more spectacular and sensational than states of mind and, because they have form, color, and motion, they are easier to describe. Thus they are common in all religions, but they do not necessarily carry with them the sense of freedom, salvation, or deliverance that is the most profound, the most satisfying and the most lasting of religious experiences. There are few who would not rather have this sense than a thousand visions.

Many attempts have been made to describe the feeling of salvation which the Buddhists call Nirvana and the Hindus call

*Moksha.* Where these descriptions are in the form of doctrines we notice that among such doctrines there is a wide variety of differences whereby students of religion are often misled. If the doctrines of Christianity are different from those of Hinduism, it does not necessarily follow that the religions are different, for more than one doctrine may describe a single state of mind, and without this state of mind the religion, as a mere collection of doctrines, has no meaning whatever; it is just as if it were a babble of unintelligible words. But doctrines differ because people have different mental backgrounds and traditions; an English person and a Chinese person may have the same feeling but they will speak of it in different ways because they are relating it to different mental contexts. It is therefore most unwise to study religion from the standpoint of doctrine *as* doctrine, for this is the purest superficiality. Doctrines and conceptual ideas vary as languages vary, but one and the same meaning may be conveyed by both English and French. Christians believe in a personal God and Buddhists do not, but as regards the true essentials of religion this difference is as superficial as the fact that in French every noun has a gender, whereas this is not so in English.

Therefore to extract the true meaning of a religious doctrine we must ask, "What does this doctrine mean in terms of a state of mind? What sort of feeling towards life and the universe would have caused a man to think in this way?" For religious experience is like the experience of beauty; indeed, it is something closely akin to feeling beauty in the whole of life instead of in a single picture, scene, image, or melody. Beethoven and Stravinsky may both arouse the sense of beauty, and they are quite as different in their own ways as Christianity and Buddhism. The important thing, however, is that they arouse that sense; we may discuss and argue over their respective "merits" till all are blue without coming to any conclusion. It would be more profitable, however, if we could take one who feels beauty in Beethoven and one who feels beauty in Stravinsky, and then consider the varying degrees of profundity in their respective feelings. But here we should be dealing with such intangible and imponderable factors that ordinary methods of criticism and discussion would be useless, and we could only judge by intuition. The same principle applies in religion, for the feeling of beauty in art or music is here the feeling of salvation. By this I do not mean freedom of moral conscience nor even the certainty of an everlasting life of bliss after death, although such things may be attained by any number of different religious systems. These elementary forms of "salvation" have much the same relation to the deeper forms as mere sensuous thrill has to the perception of beauty.

What, then, is a truly deep feeling of salvation? Insofar as this question can be answered at all, perhaps it is best to consider one of the greatest doctrines in all religion in terms of a state of mind. For this purpose the best choice is probably the Hindu or Vedanta conception of Brahman, because this is at once the simplest and the most subtle of doctrines—subtle just because it is so simple. The same doctrine is found in other systems, but Vedanta gives it the best philosophical expression. It is that all possible things, events, thoughts and qualities are aspects of a single Reality which is sometimes called the Self of the universe. In themselves these many aspects have no reality; they are real only in that each one of them is a manifestation of Brahman or the Self. To put it in another way, the true self of any given thing is Brahman and not something that belongs exclusively to the thing in question. Each individual is therefore an aspect of Brahman, and no two aspects are the same. But man's self is much more than what he considers to be his ego, his personality called John Smith or William Jones. The ego is a device or trick *(maya)* employed so that Brahman may manifest itself, and man's innermost self is therefore identical with the Self of all things. Thus if anyone wants to know what Brahman is he has just to look around, to think, to act, to be aware, to live, for all that is known by the senses, thought in the mind or felt in the heart is Brahman.

In other systems of thought Brahman has many other names—"Tao" in Chinese, and mystics the world over find similar meaning in the words "God," "Allah," "Infinite Life," "élan vital," "the Absolute," or whatever other term may be used. In fact, the intuition of the One Reality is the essence of all mystical religion, but few people understand clearly what it is to feel this intuition in oneself. We are perhaps more apt to think of this idea just as a metaphysical speculation, a more or less reasonable theory about the fundamental structure of life. Someday, we think, it might be possible for us to delve down into the deepest recesses of our souls, lay our fingers on this mysterious universal essence and avail ourselves of its tremendous powers. This, however, does not seem quite the right way to took at it. For one thing, it is not to be found only "in the deepest recesses of our souls," and for another, the word "essence" makes it sound as if it were a highly refined, somewhat gaseous or electric and wholly formless potency that somehow dwells "inside" things. But in relation to Brahman there is neither inside nor outside; sometimes it is called the principle of "nonduality" because nothing else exists beside it and nothing is excluded from it. It is to be found on the surface as much as in the depths and in the finite as much as in the infinite, for it has wisely been said that "there is nothing infinite apart from finite things." Thus it can neither be lost nor found and you cannot avail yourself of its powers any more than you can dispense with them, for all these conceptions of having and not having, of gain and loss, finite and infinite, belong to the principle of duality. Every dualism is exclusive; it is this and not that, that and not this. But Brahman as the One Reality is all-inclusive, for the Upanishads say:*

> It is made of consciousness and mind: It is made of life and vision. It is made of the earth and the waters: It is made of air and space. It is made of light and darkness: It is made of desire and peace. It is made of anger and love: It is made of virtue and vice. It is made of all that is near: It is made of all that is afar. It is made of all.

What, then, is nonduality in terms of a state of mind? How does the mystic who has realized his identity with the One Reality think and feel? Does his consciousness expand from out of his body and enter into all other things, so that he sees with others' eyes, and thinks with others' brains? Only figuratively, for the Self which is in him and in all others does not necessarily communicate to the physical brain of John Smith, mystic, what is seen by the eyes of Pei-wang, construction worker, on the other side of the earth. I do not believe that spiritual illumination is to be understood in quite this sensational way. We shall answer the question sufficiently if we can discover what is a nondualistic state of mind. Does it mean a mind in so intense a state of concentration that it contains only one thought? Strictly speaking, the mind never contains more than one thought at a time; such is the nature of thinking. But if spirituality means thinking only and always of one particular thing, then other things are excluded and this is still duality. Does it mean, then, a mind which is thinking of everything at once? Even if this were possible, it would exclude the convenient faculty of thinking of one thing at a time and would still be dualistic. Clearly these two interpretations are absurd, but there is another way of approach.

*Juan Mascaró, trans., *Himalayas of the Soul.* Translations of the principal Upanishads. (London, 1938), 89.

---

Spiritual illumination is often described as absolute freedom of the soul, and we have seen that the One Reality is all-inclusive. Is the mind of the mystic singularly free and all-inclusive? If so, it would seem that his spirituality does not depend on thinking any special kinds of thoughts, on having a particular feeling ever in the background of his soul. He is free to think of anything and nothing, to love and to fear, to be joyful or sad, to set his mind on philosophy or on the trivial concerns of the world; he is free to be both a sage and a fool, to feel both compassion and anger, to experience both bliss and agony.

And in all this he never breaks his identity with the One Reality—God, "whose service is perfect freedom." For he knows that in whatever direction he goes and in whichever of these many opposites he is engaged, he is still in perfect harmony with the One that includes all directions and all opposites. In this sense, serving God is just living; it is not a question of the way in which you live, because all ways are included in God. To understand this is to wake up to your freedom to be alive.

But is that *all*? Is it possible that spirituality can be anything so absurdly simple? It seems to mean that to attain spirituality you have just to go on living as you have always lived; all life being God, any kind of life is spiritual. You say that if the idea were not so ludicrous it would be exceedingly dangerous. First we might remind ourselves of a saying of the Chinese sage, Lao-tzu:

> When the wise man hears of the Tao, he puts it into
>     practice. . . . When the fool hears of it, he laughs
>     at it;
> Indeed, it would not be worthy to be called Tao if he
>     did not laugh at it.

The idea that any kind of life is spiritual is a terrible blow to man's pride; from the spiritual point of view it puts us on the same level as stones, vegetables, worms, and beetles; it makes the righteous man no nearer to salvation than the criminal and the sage no nearer than the lunatic. Thus if all else about the idea is folly, it is at least a powerful antidote to spiritual pride and self-reward for being a good boy; indeed, it is not something which you can *get* at all, however fierce your efforts, however great your learning and however tireless your virtue. In the spiritual world there is no top and bottom of the class; here all men and all things are equal and whatever they do can go neither up nor down. The only difference between sage or mystic and ordinary, unenlightened man is that the one realizes his identity with God or Brahman, whereas the other does not. But the lack of realization does not alter the fact.

How, then, does one attain this realization? Is it just a matter of going on living as one has lived before, knowing that one is free to do just exactly as one likes? Beware of the false freedom of doing as you like; to be really free you must also be free to do as you don't like, for if you are only free to do as you like you are still tied up in dualism, being bound by your own whims. A better way of attaining realization is to let yourself be free to be ignorant, for fools also are one with God. If you strive to attain realization and try to make yourself God, you simply become an intense egotist. But if you allow yourself freedom to be yourself, you will discover that God is not what you have to *become*, but what you *are*—in spite of yourself. For have we not heard it said a thousand times that God is always found in humble places?

"The Tao," said Lao-tzu, "is like water; it seeks the lowly level which men abhor." And while we are busy trying to add cubits to our stature so that we may reach up to heaven, we forget that we are getting no nearer to it and no further away. For "the kingdom of heaven is within you."

# Is There an Unconscious?

WHEN WE SAY THAT THE CHIEF CONTRIBUTION OF modern psychology to human knowledge is the concept of the unconscious mind, we have to be careful of our terms. For the idea of the unconscious does not belong by any means to all modern psychology, and those schools to which it does belong have somewhat different views on the subject. The concept is associated principally with the names of Freud, Jung, and Adler, but there is no one name which covers their three schools. Freud's system is psychoanalysis; Jung's is analytical psychology; Adler's is individual psychology. There is no real reason, however, why they should not all be called psychoanalysis, because if, as is frequently done, we group them under the name "modern psychology" we thereby group them with such important systems as gestalt psychology, in which the concept of the unconscious plays no part. Popularly it is believed that psychoanalysis teaches that man has an unconscious mind; this is not strictly true, for the unconscious is not to be understood as an entity or mental organism having definite location and identity. There is no actual division between the unconscious and the rest of the human organism, for it bears somewhat the same relation to the mind as the glands, liver, kidneys, etc., bear to the body: they are integral parts of the body, but we are not ordinarily conscious of them. The only difference is that the unconscious has no specific boundaries. It consists rather of the *condition of* being unaware of certain desires, impulses, tendencies, reactions, and fantasies in our mental and emotional makeup. It has its physical parallel in the condition of being unaware of various bodily organs and processes.

There appears, however, to be little or no mention of the unconscious in the world's religious, mystical, and occult philosophy. Indeed, to many students of these matters the idea is distasteful, and Freud, the father of psychoanalysis, has never been forgiven for regarding religion as a neurosis. In fact, the majority of religious people, whether of orthodox or heterodox persuasion, regard psychoanalysis in all its forms as an upstart science whose avowed object is to "debunk" all the noble impulses of humanity by ascribing them to repressed sexuality. Much of the contempt in which psychoanalysis is held is well deserved, but this should not blind us to a certain amount of gold among the dross. The trouble with this new science is not so much psychoanalysis as psychoanalysts. We might mention the professor in charge of a certain well-known clinic who devotes his life to the study of inkblot tests. The patient is made to drop a blot of ink on a piece of paper and is suddenly asked what he thinks it looks like. Being rather puzzled and humorous the patient usually grins and says something like, "Oh, it might be an elephant with warts," whereat the professor assumes a faraway expression and murmurs, "Very significant. *Most* interesting. An elephant, yes. With warts. Exceedingly interesting."

This case is not unusual, for the strange ways of psychoanalysts and psychiatrists would fill many volumes. I have heard fully qualified M.D.s discuss the case of a small boy whose propensity to bed-wetting was undoubtedly due to his unconscious identification of himself with Jupiter Pluvius. Still more significant are the gatherings of doctors and patients for summer schools where people take you by the hand, look into your eyes and ask you whether you are an extravert or an introvert. Indeed, such forms of psychology have swiftly acquired all the symptoms of crank religions. But just as there are half-wits and charlatans as well as true students in mysticism and occultism, psychology also has its heights and depths, both as to its ideas and its practitioners. There are, too, the same internal conflicts, the same bigotry, the same dogmatism, the same personal idolatry, but one could hardly expect otherwise and the mutual contempt of religion and psychology is but "the pot calling the kettle black."

In spite of all, however, psychoanalysis has a definite and valuable contribution for students of religion *in our time.* I say "in our time" because psychoanalysis is essentially a modern remedy for a modern ill; it exists for that period in human history for which the unconscious is a problem, and a problem it has been since man began to imagine that all his difficulties of soul and circumstance could be solved by the unaided power of human reason. The ancient paths of mysticism and occultism resolved the problem of the unconscious from the very beginning, even before it became a problem, for their first requirement was that man should *know himself.* Whereat he very quickly found that the huge, brute forces of nature had their counterparts in his soul, that his being was not a simple unit but a pantheon of gods and demons. In fact, all the deities of the ancient theologies were known to the initiated as the inhabitants not of Olympus but of the human soul. They were not mere products of man's imagination any more than his heart, lungs, and stomach are products of his imagination. On the contrary, they were very real forces belonging both to nature (the macrocosm), and man (the microcosm). Occultism was thus the art of living with one's gods and demons, and you had to know how to deal with them in yourself before you could deal with them in the universe. The ancients understood the laws which man must follow in order to live with them, how by love the gods would become your friends and the demons your servants. In every initiation rite it was necessary to pass through that valley of the shadow where the neophyte comes face to face with the Dweller on the Threshold and all the most terrible powers of the psyche. But the rite could only be successful if he faced them with love, recognizing them as manifestations of the same Divinity which was his own true Self. By this love he broke their spell and became a true initiate.

But man became overrational and forgot the gods and demons, relegating them to the realm of outworn superstitions. He looked for them in the skies and found only infinite spaces, dead rocks, and orbs of burning gas. He looked for them in thunder and wind and found only unintelligent forces of the atmosphere. He looked for them in woods and caverns and found only scuttling animals, creaking branches, shadows, and drafts. He thought that the gods were dead but in fact they became much more alive and dangerous because they were able to work unrecognized. For whereas the old occultists began with the principle *"know thyself,"* the rationalists began with *"rule thyself."* They chose what they considered to be a reasonable pattern of character and strove to impose it on their lives without any preliminary exploration. They forgot that it is impossible for man to behave like a sage until he has first come to terms with his inner pantheon; as a result he could only achieve a poor imitation of the sage's behavior because he had not done the necessary groundwork. For this reason the rationalist, puritanical mind is a veneer above a muck-heap, an attempt to copy greatness by wearing its clothes.

But when psychologists began to have the idea of the unconscious this was simply man's fumbling rediscovery of the lost gods and demons. Naturally experienced occultists of both East and West were inclined to smile, for to them this new force called the unconscious had never existed as such. And when people started talking about the unconscious as if it were just a repository of repressed sexuality, the occultists laughed outright, knowing that it contained far more powerful divinities than libido, who was just a little imp dancing upon the surface. It must have seemed funnier still to hear the unconscious discussed as if it were a sort of individual with secret, dark designs and an unfortunate habit of wanting and thinking in direct opposition to the conscious. For the unconscious is not an individual; it is simply that about himself which man does not know. As such it is a purely relative term, because some people know more about themselves than others. Symbolically it may be represented as an individual, for in dreams the unknown aspect of men presents itself as a woman and vice versa with women. But actually when it is said that the unconscious does this or that, it means that certain particular aspects of your internal universe are on the move without your conscious knowledge.

The concept of the unconscious is nevertheless important to *modern* students of religion and occultism in that it is a reminder of the forgotten gods and of the place where they are to be found. Too many would-be mystics and occultists try to follow the rationalist technique of imposing a discipline upon themselves without first understanding the nature of the thing to be disciplined. You have to come to terms with the gods before you can ignore them, and those who jump straight from ordinary ways of living into the complex disciplines of occultism are inviting trouble. For until those terms have been made, the gods rule us although we have a way of persuading ourselves that their often unreasonable dictates are our own free and considered choice. Thus imitation of the sage is often a device put up by the demons for our own destruction, for modem man simply does not realize that until he has been through the valley of the shadow his life is not his own. Until he looks within himself, seeks out his hidden pantheon and overcomes it by love (or what psychologists call "acceptance"), he remains its unwitting tool.

---

In all the old philosophies—Yoga, Buddhism, the Greek Mysteries, the Egyptian Mysteries—this exploring of the unknown self was the essential first step, and now the same thing is attempted by the psychoanalyst, using a different technique and terminology. That there are failures and mistakes is only to be expected, for here are men trying to work out the divine science on their own with little recourse to the experience of the ages, though to this there are a few notable exceptions. And though students of religion may be offended when religion is ascribed to repressed sexuality, it must be remembered that in many cases this may actually be true and that psychologists have had insufficient opportunities to study that comparatively rare phenomenon, the genuine mystic or occultist. For what would such a person want with psychoanalysis? The warning to the beginner, however, still stands, for unless you really know yourself, how can you say that your apparently noble aspirations are what they seem to be? Thoughts are often wolves in sheep's clothing.

Then is the first step on the path a visit to a psychoanalyst? Unfortunately the matter is not quite so easy. If you can find a *competent* analyst, perhaps, but the profession of analyst attracts many who need their own medicine more than any of their patients. The reason is that psychoanalysis has not yet had sufficient profundity of experience to judge its own results, to institute a hierarchy of "initiates" who can be trusted to say who is and is not fit to take up the profession. There is another alternative, though the professional analyst usually regards it with horror: that is to analyze yourself. It needs care and a pair of feet planted firmly on the earth, but if due regard is paid to the rules it can be done. You can follow the age-old techniques of meditation and you will often be safer in your own hands than in those of an analyst. Of course it is risky, but in these days so many people expect a "safe" way to wisdom. The way to wisdom is, however, a great deal less "safe" than the way to making a fortune; it is perhaps the riskiest and most worthwhile thing in the world, but you should not start out on it unless you are prepared to break your neck.

# That Far-Off, Divine Event

WHAT IS IT THAT TENNYSON DESCRIBED AS THAT "far-off divine event to which all creation moves"? In mystical and occult philosophy it is the return of all individual things to the divine source from which they originally came—an event which Hindu cosmology places at the end of a stupendous period of time called a *mahamanvantara,* or a "great manifestation" of Brahman. For according to Hindu and Theosophical teachings, universal activity is a succession of the days and nights of Brahman, the out-breathings and in-breathings of the One Reality of Life, whose name is derived from the Sanskrit "brih-," from which our own word "breath" is also descended. Modern science has now begun to think of time in somewhat the same terms as the ancient Hindus, for they measured these days and nights of Brahman by groups of *kalpas,* a kalpa being a mere 4,320,000,000 years. Now if these things are true, the ordinary man or woman has to accept them rather much on faith; and because it is difficult, if not impossible, for ordinary people to test their verity, and because the periods of time involved are past imagining, it will be asked whether such ideas are of the remotest practical value. For the events of which we are speaking are certainly divine and undoubtedly far off, and it may seem that the ancient Hindus were indulging in idle speculations for want of anything better to do.

For us the difficulty of this Hindu conception of the "far-off, divine event" when all things shall again become one with Brahman is that, taken at its face value, it makes the soul despair. For not only does so terrifying a period of time lie between now and the final resting of the universe in Divine Bliss, but the doctrine also goes on to say that eventually the universe will return again into a manifestation, to another, and another, and another repetition of the whole process ad infinitum. It is important to remember, however, that the ancient teachers of these doctrines often described cosmological processes in terms of time simply for the sake of explanation, whereas they should actually be understood in terms of eternity. In this sense eternity is not just everlasting time; eternity is beyond time; it is *now.* The days and nights of Brahman are spread out in time in rather the same way as a ball of thread an inch in diameter is unrolled to the length of a hundred yards. Its real state resembles the ball, but to be presented to the human mind it has to be unrolled. For our idea of time is spatial; it has length, which is a spatial dimension. But eternity has no length, and the nearest thing to it in our experience is what we call the present moment. It cannot be measured, but it is always here.

The value of this Hindu idea becomes apparent when we think of it in this way. For it means that the "far-off, divine event" is not just millions of years in the future: it is now. At this moment the universe is both manifested as a collection of separate individual things, and at the same time each of these things retains absolute unity and identity with its divine source. The object of Hindu, and for that matter of almost all Asian religion, is to awaken in man the realization of this unity and identity. In Hinduism this realization is called moksha or *kaivalya,* and in Buddhism Nirvana, and it is astonishing how seldom the West achieves any real understanding of what this condition of the spirit involves. The old nineteenth-century idea that nirvana

meant simply oblivion is now generally discredited, but some of
the conceptions that have taken its place are almost as fantastic.
Certain allowances for this misunderstanding must be made, for
just as in the West there are mature and immature conceptions
of Christianity, so in the East there are mature and immature
conceptions of Hinduism and Buddhism. In fact even some of
the canonical scriptures of the East are just as overlaid with the
interpolated comments of scribes as the Bible, even more so in
the Buddhist scriptures.

It is therefore quite common to find moksha or nirvana described as a type of trance condition in which all sense of the
separate forms and objects of the universe has vanished, to be
replaced by a state of "infinite consciousness" into which the
individual becomes absorbed even though his physical body may
continue to live on. If he ever returns out of this trance condition
it remains always in the back of his mind; the things around him
seem like the insubstantial shadows of a dream, for:

> Life, like a dome of many-colored glass, stains the white
> radiance of eternity till death tramples it to fragments. . . .

At death he merges his individuality forever into infinitude
unless he wishes to return again to the earth in order to teach
dharma (the Law) to men. But one of the principal mistakes of
Western interpretations of Asian thought is to equate Brahman
with the infinite and the realization of one's identity with Brahman as a change from finite to infinite consciousness. It is well
to remember the pertinent words of the Isa Upanishad:

> In darkness are they who worship the world alone, but in
> greatest darkness are they who worship the infinite alone.
> By a knowledge of the former we are saved from death, and
> by a knowledge of the latter we are preserved to immortality.

The highest Hindu philosophy bears the name *advaita,* which is the principle of "nonduality," meaning that Brahman is that to which nothing can be opposed as long is opposed to short, light to dark, pleasure to pain, positive to negative and infinite to finite. This also is a cardinal principle of Mahayana Buddhism, from which it is clear that neither in Hinduism or Buddhism can it be said that the highest spiritual attainment is to become merged into any kind of infinitude.

Man realizes his identity with Brahman. In other words, one cannot say that Nirvana is infinite and not finite, or vice versa, or even that it is a consciousness of unity and not diversity. Here again is an Asian conception which is little understood in the West, for it is often thought that the supreme Universal Reality of Hinduism and Buddhism has the quality of oneness as distinct from many-ness, and that realization is the knowledge that the forms and objects of the universe are in fact one, even though they appear to be many. Their seeming diversity is said to be an illusion (maya) which the wise man will overcome. But this Reality is not quite one in the sense we give to the word; to use a Vedantic expression, Reality is "one-without-a-second." In the ordinary way the idea of *one* immediately suggests the idea of many or of *none,* for the moment you have the concept of nothing you also have the concept of something, while in the same way we could not entertain the idea of many things without that of one thing. The reason for this is that the idea of oneness belongs to the multitudinous "pairs of opposites" *(dvandva)* of which life is composed, for one suggests many just as long suggests short; the two concepts are mutually essential and the one can only be known by means of the other. But Brahman or Reality is beyond opposites, being that which does not require distinction for its existence. For Brahman *is* all things, this world we see around us, together with our consciousness and the thoughts in our minds and the feelings in our hearts. To see Brahman we have just to look with our eyes, for Brahman is nothing other than what we are beholding at this moment. "So what?" you ask. "At the moment I am beholding a book. Is that anything to get excited about? Should I feel uplifted and spiritually enlightened just because this book is Brahman? I don't see anything divine and mighty about this collection of paper and printer's ink."

In view of this it will also be asked what is the difference between a sage and an ordinary ignorant man. We are accustomed to believe that a sage or mystic is one who beholds God or Brahman in all things; but if Brahman is all things, surely an ordinary man in seeing them is doing no less than the sage? This is perfectly true, but the difference between the sage and the ordinary man is that the latter fails to realize it. The reason is that because there is nothing apart from Brahman, Brahman cannot be seen in quite the ordinary way. To see things we must be able to *distinguish* them, which means that we must be able to separate them from other things or from ourselves. But with Brahman this cannot be done, for when you look at this book Brahman is looking at Brahman. We have therefore to consider how the sage comes to understand this and in what way this understanding is of practical value.

Naturally the sage does not understand it only conceptually; for him it is not just an intellectual idea, as that space is curved. A mathematician may be able to prove, in theory, that space is curved, but he cannot see it curved with his eyes, and thus the knowledge is for him purely conceptual and makes no difference to his ordinary behavior. He does not start to walk in curves; and unless he is absentminded in the way of some of his kind he does not find it impossible to go from San Francisco to New York without going through Mexico City. But for the sage the knowledge of his identity with Brahman is of immense practical importance; he knows it as well and as fully as he knows that he is alive. But this certainly does not mean that in place of himself, other people, houses, stars, hills, and trees he sees a formless, all-pervasive and infinite luminosity, which seems to be some people's idea of the Divine Reality. If such a state of consciousness were possible, it would still be dualistic, involving an utter difference between Reality and the ordinary world. It should rather be said that he feels Brahman, the force of the universe, at work in everything he does, thinks, and feels, and this gives a powerful and liberating impulse to his spirit. For he feels free and delivered, which is the precise meaning of *kaivalya*. He is freed from himself, which is the only thing that ever bound anyone, because he has let himself go. The unenlightened man keeps a tight hold on himself because he is afraid of losing himself; he can trust neither circumstances nor his own human nature; he is terrified of being genuine, of accepting himself as he is and tries to deceive himself into the belief that he is as he wishes to be. But these are the wishes, the desires that bind him, and it was such desires as these that the Buddha described as the cause of human misery.

People imagine that letting themselves go would have disastrous results; trusting neither circumstances nor themselves, which together make up life, they are forever interfering and trying to make their own souls and the world conform with preconceived patterns. This interference is simply the attempt of the ego to dominate life. But when you see that all such attempts are fruitless and when you relax the fear-born resistance to life in yourself and around you which is called egoism, you realize the freedom of union with Brahman. In fact you have always had this freedom, for the state of union with Brahman can neither be attained nor lost; all men and all things have it, in spite of themselves. It can only be realized, which is to say made real to you, by letting life live you for a while instead of trying to make yourself live life. You will soon reach the point where you will be unable to tell whether your thoughts and feelings are your own or whether life put them into you, for the distinction between yourself and life will have disappeared. If the truth be known, there never was any distinction, save in our imaginations. This is called union with Brahman, for "he that loseth his life shall find it."

# The Parable of the Cow's Tail

A FAMOUS ZEN KOAN ASKS:

When a cow goes out of its enclosure to the edge of the abyss, its horns and head and its hoofs all pass through, but why can't the tail also pass?"

Commenting on this, an old master says:

If the cow runs it will fall into the trench; If it returns it will be butchered.

That little tail is a very strange thing.

In the quest for understanding of life there comes a time when everyone is confronted with "that little tail"—the one tiny obstacle that stands in the way of complete fulfillment. We know that it is only a fraction of a hairsbreadth in thickness, and yet we feel it as a million miles wide. There is in mathematics an equation which, when drawn as a graph, appears as a curve that always nears but never touches a given line. At first the curve sweeps boldly towards that line, and the head, horns, and hoofs go clean through the gate, but, just as the tail is about to pass, the curve straightens, leaving just a fraction of an inch between itself and the line. As it moves on, that fraction grows less and less, but still curve and line do not touch, and even though it be continued for a thousand miles or a thousand million miles the gap remains, though at each successive point it becomes smaller. This curve represents the progress of human intellect towards Enlightenment, grasping more and more subtle nuances of meaning at each stage of its journey. It is as if we stood bound to illusion by a hair; to weaken it we split it with the knife of intellect, and split it again until its divisions become so fine that to make its cuts the mind must be sharpened indefinitely. Yet however much we split this hair, the sum total of its divisions is not a whit thinner than the original hair, for the more fragile we make our bonds, the more is their number.

Philosophically this condition is known as infinite regression, and psychologically it is that mad, exasperating state that must always precede the final experience of awakening. We can demonstrate this by the famous triangle puzzle of Mahayana philosophy. The two base points of this triangle represent the pairs of opposites which confront us at every moment of our experience—subject and object, I and you, positive and negative, something and nothing. The apex represents the relation, the meaning between them, the principle that gives them reality, the One as distinct from the Many. But the moment we set this One apart from the Many we create yet another pair of opposites, thus initiating a process which will continue indefinitely with ever-increasing complications. In the Bhagavad Gita we are told to stand aside from our thoughts and feelings, to realize that they are not the Self and learn that the Self is not the actor in actions but the Spectator of actions. But why not stand aside yet again from this first standing aside and perceive that it is not the Self that stands aside, for the Self performs no action? This, too, may continue forever.

The first step in Buddhism is Right Motive, and to attain Enlightenment it is said that we must do away with selfish desire. But if we have selfish desire in the beginning, surely the desire to get rid of it is also selfish. We desire to be rid of our selfishness for a selfish reason, and again we may easily have a selfish reason for getting rid of the selfish reason for wanting to be selfless. An even more fundamental illustration of the problem may be found in the simplest statement of Eastern philosophy, namely, that there is only one Reality and that all diversity is illusion. This is a statement which almost all students of Eastern wisdom take very much for granted: it is the first thing they learn but in fact it is about almost all there is to learn, for the rest is mere embroidery. It is the central principle of Vedanta, Mahayana, and Taoism alike: there are no two principles in the universe; there is only Brahman, Tathata, or Tao, and Enlightenment is just the realization of one's identity with it. But here the complications begin and the cow's tail gets stuck in the gate, for the moment we think, "This is Tao" or "That is Tao" we immediately make a distinction between Tao and this and that. Furthermore, as soon as we think that the object of religion is to identify ourselves with the Tao, we create the dualism of the Tao and ourselves that are to be identified with it. Dualism appears the moment we make an assertion or a denial about anything; as soon as we think that *This is That* or *This is not That* we have the distinction between *This* and *That*. And even when we say that in Reality there are no distinctions, we have the opposition of Reality and distinctions.

Moreover, let us consider this problem: if there is only Tao, how can there be any divergence from it? If there is only one Reality, our thoughts, enlightened or unenlightened, must be it. There can be no distinction between Reality and illusion if there is only Reality. Whether you can concentrate your thoughts or not, whether they are of compassion or hatred, whether you are thinking about Buddhism or chewing your nails, you cannot by any means diverge from the Tao. You may love life or you may loathe it, yet your loving and loathing are themselves manifestations of life. If you seek union with Reality your very seeking is Reality, and how can you say that you have ever lost union?

To put it in another way: it is said that to be enlightened we must live in the eternal. Now, that infinitely small and therefore infinitely great point of time is called the present moment. The universe exists only in that moment, and it is said that the wise man moves with it, clinging neither to the past nor to the future, making his mind like the mirror that reflects everything instantly as it comes before it, yet making no effort to retain the reflection when the object is removed. "The perfect man," says Chuang-tzu, "employs his mind as a mirror. It grasps nothing; it refuses nothing. It receives, but does not keep."

Yet, when the matter is carefully considered, we find that this is a description, not of what we should do, but of what we cannot help doing in any case. For whether we think of the past or the future, and whatever we think about either of them, our thoughts exist in and partake of the eternal Now; otherwise they would not exist at all. We cannot separate ourselves from this present moment, and if we imagine that Enlightenment consists simply in living in the present, in thinking only about what is going on now, we find ourselves in the dualism of now and then. The point is that we can only think of what is going on now, even if we are thinking of the past or the future. For our thoughts about past and future are going on now, and we are thinking them. There is only one Reality! Therefore it will be asked: "Is Enlightenment simply to live and think like any ignorant fool, not bothering about philosophy, mysticism, or morality, knowing that whatever you do you cannot get out of harmony with the Tao?"

If we answer, "Yes," we assert; if we say, "No," we deny. The tail is still caught in the gate. But if you think that you will attain Enlightenment by living like an ignorant fool, you are still caught in the dualism of the *you* that must attain enlightenment. Indeed, there is no prescription for enlightenment, for as soon as we start saying that it is this or it is not this, we try to make two realities in the universe instead of one. In fact, you can think about philosophy, or about eating and drinking, you can love mankind, you can hate it, you can do as you like, you can do as you don't like, you can discipline yourself, you can run wild, you can seek wisdom, you can ignore it, but you can't diverge from the Tao, for everything, anything, and nothing is Tao. *Is* it? Beware of that "is." The sting is in the tail.

# The Second Immortal

ONCE UPON A TIME THERE WAS A MAN WHO LIVED much as other men live. He had a wife and three children and a shop in the Street of Happy Sparrows where he sold cakes, vegetables, and sweet pickles. He rose at dawn and went to bed at sunset; he ate rice three times a day; he smoked two pipes of tobacco in the hour; he talked of buying and selling with his neighbors; he picked his teeth after eating and had his wife scratch his back in the noonday heat. In spring he watched the young grass peeping out from behind the stones; in summer he lifted an eye at the lazy clouds; in autumn he followed the leaves that danced in the wind; and in winter he woke to see the tracks of birds in the snow. And in all seasons, between talking and smoking and selling cakes, he chewed watermelon seeds and amused himself by plaiting straw ropes round his toes.

One day, when he went to burn incense at the Temple of Amiable Dragons, his friend the priest approached him, saying: "You are getting on in years and your eldest son is of an age to take care of your shop. It would not be proper for a man such as you to spend the rest of your days in empty activities, for you will go to the grave as insignificantly as old refuse is flung into the river."

"Such being the lot of man," answered the cakeseller, "how can I complain?"

"So many are mere vegetables." said the priest. "But if you are willing to take the trouble you can find yourself a place among the Immortals."

"And who," asked the cakeseller, "are the Immortals?"

"They are those who do not depend on their own power to keep themselves alive. Man is a small creature whose life is like a snowflake. But the wind blows on forever; the sun and moon eternally maintain their courses and the rivers have flowed since time began. The Immortals are they who learn the secrets of these things; instead of relying on their own resources, they allow themselves to be maintained and directed by that which maintains and directs the wind, the sun, the moon, and the rivers."

"But how can one become an Immortal?"

"You will have to find an Immortal to teach you," said the priest. "I am not wise enough."

"Well," said the cakeseller. "I must find one. But there are so many people in the world, and how can one recognize an Immortal?"

"That should not be difficult," answered the priest. "It is said that their breath is operated by the wind; that the sun gives them the light of the right eye and the moon of the left; that their shouting is assisted by the thunder, their whispering by the murmuring waves and their laughter by the mountain streams. The earth, it is said, maintains their flesh, while their bones and vital juices are supplied by the rocks and the rains. Their thoughts and moods are directed by the coming and going of the seasons and the elements, and having such mighty ones as the movers of all their functions they are said to be free from all the ordinary limitations and more powerful even than the gods."

"Such a strange being," observed the cakeseller, "should be easy to recognize," and immediately he returned home, set his affairs in order, instructing his eldest son in the care of the shop, and the same evening left the city on his journey in search of an Immortal. After many weeks upon the road he came to a hut inhabited by an ancient personage of severe aspect who seemed to him to be at least two hundred years old. His white beard caressed the upper part of his shoes and the top of his head glistened like the elbows of an old coat. Noticing his venerable appearance, and also the many volumes of the classics with which he was surrounded, the cakeseller at once approached him and begged for instruction, thinking that surely this must be an Immortal, for he was the most aged person he had ever seen. "It is a long time," said the venerable one, "since my advice was asked upon anything, for this is a dissolute age, and the mastery of life is not understood by those who fail to observe the forty-eight precepts and fail to avoid the ninety-one indiscretions. Sit down, and I will instruct you in the words of the ancient sages." Whereupon he began to read from the classics, and the cakeseller sat and listened until the sun went down. And on the following day he read yet more, and again on the next day and the next and the next, and so on, until the cakeseller almost lost count of time. And he was instructed and made to discipline himself in the eight virtuous deeds, the twenty-nine laudable thoughts, the one hundred and eight ceremonial observances, the forty-two marks of superior character, the thirty-seven acts of filial piety and the four hundred and three propitiations of ill-disposed spirits. And all the while the cakeseller grew in righteousness and high-minded conduct, and was disposed to believing himself well on the way to immortality. But one day he remembered suddenly that he had now been with the venerable scholar for some twenty years; the days of his life were growing shorter and yet he knew nothing of the secrets of sun, moon, rivers, wind, and the elements. At this he was filled with agitation, and in the night set out upon the road again.

---

After some weeks of wandering in the mountains he came upon a cave where a strange being sat at the entrance. His limbs were like the trunk of a gnarled pine, his hair like wisps of smoke drifting on the wind and his eyes staring and fiery like those of a snake. Duly impressed, the cakeseller again begged for instruction.

"Immortals," said this person, "have the wind as their breath, and to learn this you must cultivate the art of the Expansive Lungs. But this cannot be learned by such as you who chew melon seeds and smoke two pipes an hour and eat three meals a day. If you would have the wind as your breath, you must eat but one grain of rice in a day and drink one cup of water. You must clear the smoke from your windpipe, and learn to breathe but twice in a day. Only then will your lungs be able to contain the wind."

So the cakeseller sat down at the mouth of the cave, ate but one grain of rice and drank but one cup of water a day. And under the instructions of the sage he was made to lessen and lessen the speed of his breath till he thought his eyes would proceed from their sockets and the drums of his ears disturb all the birds of the forest with their bursting. But for many years he practiced until he did indeed breathe but twice a day, at the end of which he saw that his body was as a skeleton hung with skin as spiderwebs cover the branches of a bush, and with a display of exceedingly ill-regulated conduct he fled from the cave.

For many more months he searched for an instructor, and finding none began to wonder whether he had perhaps not persevered enough with his teacher. So he began to make his way back to the mountains. On the way he caught up with an itinerant trader who carried a pole over his shoulder to which was attached a bundle containing an assortment of pots, beads, combs, dolls, kitchen utensils, writing materials, seeds, scissors, and sticks of incense. For a while they kept each other company, conversing on idle matters such as the state of the crops, the best ways of driving out fleas, the pleasures of soft rainfall and the various kinds of charcoal useful for making fires. At length the cakeseller told the trader of his desire to find an Immortal who could instruct him and asked whether he knew of any such person. "Have a melon seed," said the trader, offering him a handful. "Indeed, I regret I cannot eat melon seeds," cried the cakeseller, "for if I chew them it will take away my power of Expansive Lungs." The trader shrugged his shoulders, and for a while they walked on in silence, broken only by the cracking of melon seeds between the trader's teeth—a sound which filled the cakeseller with a variety of emotions. On the one hand he began to feel an urge to break his discipline, and once more feel that eminently satisfying crack of seeds between the teeth; on the other he felt he should persist in his search and again ask the trader about the Immortals. Perhaps, he thought, the trader had never heard of Immortals, but it might be that he would recognize such beings if he knew what they were like. "I was wondering," said the cakeseller, "whether in your journeyings you have happened to meet with anyone of strange and powerful aspect, whose breath is operated by the wind, whose right and left eyes are given light by the sun and moon respectively, whose shouting is assisted by the thunder, whispering by the murmuring waves and laughter by the mountain streams; whose flesh is maintained by the earth, whose bones and vital juices are supplied by the rocks and the rains, and whose thoughts and moods are directed by the coming and going of the seasons and the elements."

"Oh yes," answered the trader, "I have seen many such beings. Why, I believe that two of them are making their way along this road."

"What!" cried the cakeseller. "On this very road? Let us hurry so that we can catch up with them!" And so they increased their pace, and when night fell they did not pause to rest, for the cake-seller persuaded the trader that it would be well to gain upon them by a night's journey. At sunrise they found themselves on the top of a hill from which they could see the road ahead for many miles, but as they looked down upon it there was no one anywhere to be seen.

"It may be," said the cakeseller, "that we overtook them during the night."

Whereat they looked behind, and again a view of many miles showed them an empty road. At this the cakeseller was very sad.

"They must have taken a side-track into the mountains," he said, "for it seems that we are the only people on this road."

"Oh," said the trader, "I forgot to tell you. When they go about in pairs one of them is always invisible. You are looking for two men travelling together. Let us look again."

Once more the cakeseller gazed up the road and down the road, but saw no other man upon it than his companion, the trader.

"No," sighed the cakeseller, "we have missed them. I see neither two nor one."

"Are you sure?" replied the trader. "I really believe I can see one. Look again."

"No," said the cakeseller, "I see no man on the road at all, excepting yourself."

At this the trader began to laugh, and as he laughed it seemed to the cakeseller that his laughter was like the sound of a mountain stream.

"You!" he exclaimed. "Are you an Immortal? But you look like an ordinary man!"

"Indeed," laughed the trader, "I must confess it. You see, I have to go about in disguise, for otherwise I should be followed all over the place, which would be most inconvenient."

"But your invisible companion," asked the cakeseller, "is he also here? Does he look like an Immortal? Describe him to me."

"Surely," answered the trader. "His breathing is operated by the wind but you do not notice it; the light of his right and left eyes is given by the sun and moon, but you do not see it; his shouting is of the thunder, his whispering of the waves, and his laughter of the mountain streams, but you do not hear it; his flesh is maintained by the earth, and his bones and vital juices by the rocks and rains, but you do not understand it; his thoughts and moods are directed by the coming and going of the seasons and the elements, but you are not aware of it. He does not rely on his own resources; he allows himself to be maintained and directed by that which maintains and directs the wind, the sun, the moon, and the rivers, but you do not recognize it."

"Marvelous indeed must he be to look upon!" exclaimed the cakeseller. "Please ask him to become visible so that I can understand his secrets."

"You had better ask yourself," replied the trader. "Only you have the power to make him visible. There is a magic by which you can make him appear."

"Tell me about it."

"The magic," answered the trader, "is this: in spring to watch the young grass peeping out between the stones; in summer to lift an eye at the lazy clouds; in autumn to follow the leaves that dance in the wind; in winter to wake and find the tracks of birds in the snow. To rise at dawn and go to sleep at sunset; to eat rice three times in a day; to talk of buying and selling with one's neighbors; to chew the seeds of water melon and to plait straw ropes around the toes."

And at this the cakeseller discovered the second Immortal.

---

# The Problem of Faith and Works in Buddhism

I T   I S   G E N E R A L L Y   A S S U M E D   T H A T   P H I L O S O P H I C
Buddhism, and especially that form of it expressed in the Pali
Canon, is par excellence the way to salvation or illumination by
self-help. For in the philosophy attributed to Gautama by the
earliest records no place is given to a God or gods who can assist
man in the development of spiritual life; the existence of such
divine beings is not denied—it is ignored on the ground that no
power on earth or in heaven can interfere with another's karma.
And *karma* (in Pali, *kamma)* is a very inclusive term, for primar-
ily it means "action" or "doing," though in a secondary sense it
has come to mean the law of cause and effect—a sense which has
been much overemphasized by Western theosophical interpretations. But it would seem that original Buddhism does not only
set aside the possibility of interference with karma for the reason
that it is impossible to separate a cause from its effect (in the
Christian sense of absolution). It also rejects the possibility of
divine intervention at the causal end of the process, having no
parallel to the Christian concept of Grace. In Christianity there is
no human power that can, of its own resources, make for righteousness and salvation, for by reason of original sin it is impossible for man to move upwards without the gift of divine Grace.

Buddhism, however, would appear to be a method of lifting oneself up by one's own belt, for according to a famous passage in
the *Mahaparinibbana-sutta* (v. ii, 27–35), we are advised, "Be ye
lamps unto yourselves. Be ye a refuge unto yourselves. Take to
yourselves no other refuge."

Both Hinayana and Mahayana Buddhism in the historical development of their philosophy and practice have, for the most
part, kept to this principle of absolute self-reliance. If any faith
was involved, it was faith in one's own capacity to work out one's
own salvation, and faith in the ability of Buddhism to supply the
necessary method. In the Hinayana system the method was to
exhaust the process of karma by perceiving the fundamental unreality of the individual (*atta*) who sets karma in motion. The
Mahayana followed a variation of the same method, but, under
the influence of Brahmanic thought, supplemented the idea of
individual unreality with the concept of a universal, nondual Reality similar to the Vedantist idea of Brahman. In one sense this
Reality, called by such names as *Tathata, Shunyata,* and *Dharma-
kaya,* was beyond karma *(akarma),* and thus the realization that
it alone existed involved deliverance from the toils of karma, even
though one might continue to live in the "world of birth-and-
death." But the radical nondualism of, say, the *Lankavatara-sutra*
refused even to make any absolute distinction between karma
and akarma, the world of illusion and the principle of Reality, the
transient, separate individual and the eternal, undifferentiated
"Suchness" *(Tathata):*

> There is no Nirvana except where is Samsara; there is no
> Samsara except where is Nirvana; for the condition of exis-
> tence is not of a mutually-exclusive character. Therefore,
> it is said that all things are non-dual as are Nirvana and
> Samsara.*

*D.T. Suzuki, trans., *Lankavatara Sutra,* (London, 1932), 67.

The problem of faith and works in Buddhism, as we shall discuss it, will be entirely in terms of the Mahayana school. To understand its doctrinal and psychological background we must pay particular attention to the Mahayana doctrine of nonduality, bearing also in mind that only in Mahayana has a way of salvation by faith arisen. Our attention will be directed, however, to doctrinal and psychological aspects of the problem rather than historical, for we cannot say precisely whether the historical development of the way of faith came as a logical result of certain philosophic trends or as an answer to a natural human need. Furthermore, the historical aspect of the problem is complicated by our uncertainty as to the exact age of many of the important sutras involved. But we do know that the way of faith developed quite early in Mahayana history, playing an important role in the works of such early patriarchs of the school as Nagarjuna, Ashvaghosha, and Vasubandhu.

Mahayana philosophy is centered upon two closely related ideas. The first, descended from Vedanta, is that Enlightenment (the Buddhist life-goal) consists of an inner realization of nonduality. All those things upon which unenlightened man depends for his happiness are dual, and thus conditioned by their opposites. Life cannot be had without death, pleasure without evil. We cannot, therefore, depend for our ultimate salvation and security upon any one aspect of a given pair of opposites (dvandva), for the two are as essential to each other as back and front are essential to the totality of any object. Thus, while we look to such limited states for our salvation, we are involved in a world of ups and downs which goes under the general name of Samsara, the wheel of birth and death.

From the beginning, the purpose of Buddhism was to find deliverance from this wheel, to discover the state of Nirvana, differing from these limited states by being eternal, unchanging, and subject to no ups and downs. In the Pali Canon there is no special emphasis upon the nonduality of Nirvana. It is here something quite outside and different from Samsara—an escape. But the Mahayana Nirvana is described in much the same language as the Upanishads describe Brahman, the "One-without-a-second." Here Nirvana is the experience that differs from all these limited experiences by *having no opposite*. The Mahayana sutras are at such pains to stress the nonduality of Nirvana and Enlightenment (*bodhi*) that they do not even allow Nirvana to be opposed to Samsara, or Enlightenment to be opposed to Ignorance (*avidya*). To the fully enlightened man, Samsara *is* Nirvana; ordinary, everyday experience of the world of opposites is for him transformed into the supreme spiritual experience of deliverance or freedom.

The second important principle of Mahayana is the Bodhisattva-ideal. In one sense the Bodhisattva is a lesser Buddha. In another, he is one who, by patient striving throughout countless incarnations, has attained the right to Nirvana, but who postpones final entry into its eternal rest in order to come back into the world and work for the liberation of "all sentient beings." But this rather picturesque view of the Bodhisattva is actually taken from the Hinayana standpoint. Nirvana is still an *escape* from Samsara, even though the Bodhisattva has temporarily renounced it. But from the thoroughgoing Mahayana standpoint, the Bodhisattva-ideal is the necessary consequence of a philosophy denying the duality of Nirvana and Samsara. The Bodhisattva has no need to escape from Samsara because he realizes that it is Nirvana. Thus, to quote the *Lankavatara-sutra* again,

> those who, afraid of sufferings rising from the discrimination of birth-and-death, seek for Nirvana, do not know that

birth-and-death and Nirvana are not to be separated the one from the other; and, seeing that a things subject to discrimination have no reality, imagine that Nirvana consists in the future annihilation of the senses and their fields. They are not aware . . . of the fact Nirvana is the Alayavijnana (universal) mind. . . .*

But whatever the view of Nirvana, the Bodhisattva is the savior, the one who makes vows *(pranidhana)* to postpone any final withdrawal from the world until he has seen all living things liberated and raised to the level of his own understanding. Thus, in a number of Buddhist sects, the monk repeats daily the following vows to identify himself with the Bodhisattva-ideal:

> How innumerable sentient beings are, I vow to save
>   them all;
> How inexhaustible our evil passions are, I vow to
>   exterminate them;
> How immeasurable the holy doctrines are, I vow to
>   study them;
> How inaccessible the path of Buddhas is, I vow to
>   attain it.†

But it will be noted that, although the monk vows to save all sentient beings, he does not seem to expect anyone to save him. The remainder of his vows are firm affirmations of self-help, and this is in line with the main trend of Mahayana philosophy and practice in all but the popular sects, which have put the Bodhisattvas in the position of saviors to be worshipped and relied upon almost exactly as the Christian relies upon the saving power

*Trans. *Suzuki,* 55.
†D. T. Suzuki, *Essays in Zen Buddhism,* Vol. 1, p. 323.

of the Christ. Thus there would seem here to be a huge inconsistency between popular and philosophic Buddhism in the Mahayana school. The purpose here, however, is to show that this inconsistency is more apparent than real.

In modern China and Japan, by far the most popular form of Buddhism is a way of salvation by faith. It has attained its most radical and interesting development in Japan, but, as we have seen, its origins are in India, far back in the early days of Mahayana history. Most students of Buddhism are at a loss to find any true similarity of purpose between these popular cults and the highly self-reliant Buddhism of Gautama and philosophic Mahayana. They are generally regarded as a mere degeneration of the creed, a pure concession to unregenerate human nature, which demands supernatural beings to achieve what men are too lazy and too frightened to achieve for themselves. There is no doubt whatever that there are plenty of lazy and frightened human beings, and that an easy method of salvation by faith would naturally appeal to them, especially in the more extreme forms which altogether discount the efficacy of works. But there are other considerations, and from a certain point of view these very extreme forms become full of the deepest interest. Here let it be said that I owe this point of view to Dr. D.T. Suzuki, who made a particularly suggestive study of the philosophy and psychology underlying the Buddhism of faith in his essay, "The Shin Sect of Buddhism," (*Eastern Buddhist*, Vol. VII, nos. 3–4, July, 1939). But as yet he has made no thorough study of the psychological relations of the way of faith and the way of works. This seems to me a very necessary line of inquiry, because I believe that Western students of Christian background can never really understand the Buddhism of works unless they approach it through the Buddhism of faith, itself so close to Christian belief.

Generally speaking, the Buddhism of faith is founded upon the *Sukhavati-vyuha* which, so far as we know, was compiled some three hundred years after Gautama's death. The *Sukhavati-vyuha* tells of one Dharmakara, who, in some immeasurably distant age, made forty-eight vows concerning the liberation of sentient beings. Before making these vows he had devoted himself, for an equally incomprehensible span of time, to innumerable good works, thus acquiring for himself a store of merit sufficient to give abundant aid to the whole world. But he renounced the reward of Highest Attainment due to him for these works, in order that he might preside over the Buddha-land *(buddha-kshetra)* of Sukhavati, the Western Paradise, and there watch over the world until all living beings had been born into his Pure Land and thus assured of final illumination. From then on he was known as the Budda Amitabha (Boundless Light) or Amitayus (Eternal Life). The Chinese form of the name is *O-mi-to-fo,* and the Japanese is *Amida,* by which he is most generally known. In the second part of the sutra it is declared that those who, in complete faith, turn towards Amida and repeat his name will be born after death into the Pure Land.

But it is hard to find in the sutra itself sufficient ground for some of the later interpretations put upon it, and it was not until the time of the Japanese Amidist Shinran Shonin that there evolved a real philosophy of salvation by pure faith. In the sutra, Amida is able to transfer his merit to others because, according to the philosophy represented by the *Avatamsaka-sutra* each single atom contains in itself the whole universe. Therefore, what is done by one individual affects all others; if one man raises himself, he raises at the same time the whole universe. But here Amida is not the sole source of merit as the Christian God is the sole source of goodness. In early Mahayana the transference of merit *(parina mana)* is a process that may operate mutually between all beings, and, though the individual is helped by sharing Amida's merit, he is yet able to acquire merit by his own unaided efforts, thus adding his own contribution to a universal store. Thus, in the *Sukhavati-vyuha* the possibility of self-help is by no means excluded, and Amida remains one among many Buddhas; he is not yet raised to the position of sole source of light and life and made the personification par excellence of the final, supreme Reality. His distinction is just that he has made a particularly large contribution to the store of merit in which all may share, and has put his Buddha-land at the disposal of all who seek it in faith. There is still the difference between "*in* faith" and "*by* faith."

The growth of a cult around Amida was supported by a prevalent view that in this dark cycle *(kali yuga)* of history it is impossible for anyone to attain Enlightenment here on earth, although some progress might be made towards it; hence the advantage of being reborn into a realm unencumbered by the snares and impurities of earthly life in its dark cycle. And here we are able to note either a rationalization of pure laziness or else the growth of what Christianity calls the conviction of sin, the realization of man's impotence apart from God. There is, moreover, a remarkable parallel to this gradual break from the legalistic, ethical self-reliance of Buddhism in St. Paul's revolt against the Jewish law—and for similar psychological reasons. Thus, in the seventh chapter of his Epistle to the Romans St. Paul writes, "Nay, I had not known sin, but by the law: for I had not known lust, except the law had said, Thou shalt not covet. But sin, taking occasion by the commandment, wrought in me all manner of concupiscence." In just the same way there were Buddhists who found that the rigid morality of monkhood, with its insistence on the negative precept, served only to aggravate the inner desire for vice. They

There are two principal features of Shinran's religion. The first is his conception of parinamana, or merit transference. For him, Amida was the sole and original source of merit. Birth in the Pure Land was no longer a question of directing ones' own store of merit toward Amida—as a strictly accurate reading of the *Sukhavati-vyuha* would indicate. Shinran turned the sense of the words, making birth in the Pure Land dependent on Amida's turning his store of merit towards the individual. The second feature arises from the first, and is the doctrine of pure faith. According to Shinran, no possible human merit could ever earn the tremendous right of birth in the Pure Land, and to imagine that so great a blessing could ever be claimed as the just reward for human effort was to him the height of spiritual pride. In the light of Amida's infinite compassion *(karuna)*, all beings, whether worms, demons, saints, or sinners, were equally deserving of love, as if Amida would say, "I have the same feeling for the high as for the low, for the just as for the unjust, for the virtuous as for the depraved, for those holding sectarian views and false opinions as for those whose beliefs are good and true." Those who would put faith in Amida must therefore offer themselves to him just as they are, not imagining that the Pure Land can ever be a reward for human virtue. Amida's love is not to be earned; it is as much universal property as the sun, moon, and stars—something to be accepted with humility and gratitude, but never measured against human merit. Thus Shinran said:

> You are not to imagine that you would not be greeted by Amida in his Land because of your sinfulness. As ordinary beings you are endowed with all kinds of evil passions and destined to be sinful. Nor are you to imagine that you are assured of birth in the Pure Land because of your goodness.

As long as your jiriki sense is holding you, you would never be welcomed to Amida's true Land of Recompense.*

All that is necessary is to give up forever any idea of attaining merit by one's own power, and then to have faith that one is accepted by the compassion of Amida from the very beginning, no matter what one's moral condition. One must even give up the idea that faith itself is achieved by self-power, for faith, too, is Amida's gift. Thus man as man becomes spiritually passive and, by Amida's grace, lets the eternal love flow into him and save him just as he is, symbolizing his faith by repeating the *Nembutsu,* the formula *Namu Amida Butsu* (Hail, Amida Buddha!). According to the *Anjin-ketsujo-sho:*

> To understand the Vow means to understand the Name, and to understand the Name is to understand that when Amida, by bringing to maturity his Vow and Virtue (or Deed) in the stead of all beings, effected their rebirth *even prior to their actual attainment.*† [italics mine]

The fact that Amida himself is the sole source of grace is further stressed in this passage quoted from Shinran in the *Tannisho* (chapter 8):

> The Nembutsu is non-practice and non-goodness for its devotee. It is non-practice because he does not practise it at his own discretion, and it is non-goodness because he does not create it at his own discretion. All is through Amida's power alone, not through our own power, which is in vain.‡

*Suzuki, *Eastern Buddhist,* VII, 2, 53.
†*ibid.,* 249. The *Anjin* is a work by an unknown author, see p. 248.
‡*Tannisho,* translated by Ryukyo Fujimoto (Kyoto, 1932), p. 10.

At first sight it would seem that the efficacy of Shin depends upon certain supernatural sanctions of a kind that ordinary jiriki Buddhists would have great difficulty in believing. Such difficulties will always be experienced while Shin is studied in terms of its theology, for to anyone but a Christian it would seem the merest wishful thinking. For it amounts to this: that it is possible to become virtually a Buddha by pure faith. According to Suzuki:

> Being born in Amida's Land means no more than attaining enlightenment—the two terms are entirely synonymous. The ultimate end of the Shin life is enlightenment and not salvation.*

Thus Shin devotees refer to their dead as *Mi hotoke,* or "Honorable Buddhas." But as soon as we examine the *psychology* of Shin as distinct from its *theology,* it becomes possible to relate it to the deepest experiences of Mahayana as expressed, for instance, in the *Lankavatara-sutra* and in some of the writings of Zen teachers, notably the *Lin-chi-lu* (Japanese, *Rinzai-roku*). For we have to ask not what Shin believes, but what are the causes and results of that belief in terms of inner feeling, of those inner spiritual experiences which words alone can never fully communicate.

For example, let us take the case of any person acutely aware of his shortcomings, his fears, desires, and passions, his lack of insight, and of any sense of union or harmony with the life of the universe—in fact, just such a man as Shinran. Then someone tells him that, if only he will open his eyes and see it, he is a Buddha (is saved by Amida) just as he is, and that any attempt to make

*D.T. Suzuki, *Eastern Buddhist,* VII, 264. By "salvation" Suzuki means simply birth into Amida's Paradise after death, using the word in its eschatological rather than mystical sense. In the latter sense, salvation would be almost synonymous with Enlightenment.

himself into a Buddha by his own ingenuity is rank spiritual pride. By adopting jiriki he is ignoring what is offered to him from the very beginning by the laws of the universe, and is trying to manufacture it for himself, so that he can take the credit for having earned it. When we say that a man is a Buddha just as he is, what does this mean in terms of psychology? It means that he is divine *or fundamentally acceptable* just as he is, whether saint or sinner, sage or fool. In Amidist language we would say that he is accepted for birth in the Pure Land by Amida's compassion, which is "no respecter of persons"—in other words, that man is given the sense of freedom to be what he is at this and any moment, free to be both the highest and the lowest that is in him. This results at once in a great relaxation of psychic tension. All self-powered striving and contriving *(hakarai)* is set aside in the realization that Buddhahood can neither be attained nor got rid of because it alone *is.* For, in Mahayana nondualism, the Buddha principle, Tathata (Suchness), *has* no opposite and is the only Reality. And while the *Anjin-ketsujo-sho:* says that Amida effected our rebirth into the Pure Land "even prior to actual attainment," the *Lankavatara-sutra* says that, if they only realized it, all beings are in Nirvana from the very beginning. Here are two doctrines, but one psychological experience.

In practical terms this experience is one of exhilarating spiritual freedom, amounting almost to the sanctification of ordinary, everyday life. For, when man feels free to be all of himself, there is a magic in every littlest act and thought. Thus the Zen poet Hokoji says:

How wondrous strange and how miraculous, this—I draw water and I carry fuel.

One cannot resist quoting Herbert from the Christian standpoint:

All things of Thee partake; Nothing can be so mean
But with this tincture "For Thy Sake" Shall not grow
   bright and clean.
A servant with this clause Makes drudgery divine;
Who sweeps a room as for Thy laws Makes that and
   the action fine. . . .
This is the famous stone That turneth all to gold,
For that which God doth touch and own Can not for
   less be told.

This experience may be clarified and related more closely to
the *jiriki* way by further consideration of the *Lankavatara-sutra*
and the writings of certain Zen teachers. It will now be clear
that Shinran's faith has a right to be considered as philosophic
Mahayana expressed in rather colorful, symbolic imagery, even
though it appears to be quite dualistic in conception. Philosophic
Mahayana would not allow the dualism of self and other, man
and Amida; but, if it is followed far enough, Shin arrives in experience at what Mahayana states in philosophy—although complete nonduality is actually beyond philosophic description.
Furthermore, the *Lankavatara-sutra* insists that Samsara, the
world of life and death, is Nirvana, and Samsara just as it is, with
all its pain and suffering. So, too, Shinran insists that we are saved
by Amida just as we are, with all our imperfections. In other
words, ordinary men are Buddhas just as they are, and, according
to Hui-neng, of the Zen school, those whom we call Buddhas are
simply those who understand this truth. Thus it is often re-
marked in Zen literature that one's "ordinary thoughts" or "everyday mind" is Enlightenment (satori). I quote a peculiarly
suggestive passage from the *Rinzai-roku:*

You must not be artful. Be your ordinary self . . . *You yourself as you are—that is Buddha Dharma.* I stand or I sit; I

array myself or I eat; I sleep when I am fatigued. The ignoramus will deride me but the wise man will understand.*

And further on the text states, "Wherefore it is said that the everyday mind is the true law."

Suzuki translates another passage from this text to the same effect; here Rinzai says:

> The truly religious man has nothing to do but go on with his life as he finds it in the various circumstances of this worldly existence. He rises quietly in the morning, puts on his dress and goes out to his work. When he wants to walk, he walks; when he wants to sit, he sits. He has no hankering after Buddhahood, not the remotest thought of it. How is this possible? A wise man of old days says, If you strive after Buddhahood by any conscious contrivances, your Buddha is indeed the source of eternal transmigration.†

This kind of writing is very easily misunderstood, for one would naturally ask, "If ordinary life is Nirvana and ordinary thoughts are Enlightenment, whatever is Buddhism about, and what can it possibly teach us, other than to go on living exactly as we have lived before?" Before trying to answer this, we must quote two *mondo,* or Zen dialogues. The first is from the *Mumonkan* (XIX):

> Joshu asked Nansen, "What is the Tao?" "Usual life," answered Nansen, "is the very Tao." "How can we accord with it?" "If you *try* to accord with it, you will get away from it."‡

*Essays in Zen Buddhism, 11, p. 260.
†I follow Sohaku Ogata's translation, *Essays in Zen Buddhism, 1,* p. 12.
‡Suzuki's translation, p. 186.

The looks very much like pure *tariki* psychology. Then Suzuki gives the following from Bokushu (Mu-chou):

A monk asked him, "We have to dress and eat every day, and how can we escape from all that?" Bokushu replied, "We dress, we eat." "I do not understand." "If you don't understand, put on your dress and eat your food."

Clearly the monk's question involves much more than mere dressing and eating, which stands for life in Samsara as a whole— "the trivial round, the common task."

Applying philosophy to this more direct language, we find that the Zen teachers are demonstrating that Samsara, just as it is, is Nirvana, and that man, just as he is, is Buddha. Zen does not say so as a rule, because the terms, *Nirvana* and *Buddha,* are concepts which do not move the soul deeply and lead easily to mere intellectualism. Zen wants us to *feel* nonduality, not just to think it, and therefore when we say, "Nirvana is Samsara," we are joining two things together that were never in need of being joined. For both Zen and Shin aim, in different ways, to effect a psychological or spiritual state that moves the whole being, not the head alone. They are trying to set us free within ourselves, and to make us at home with ourselves and with the universe in which we live. This freedom is known when we give up "contriving" and accept ourselves as we are, but it does not seem to me that the experience can be effective unless there has first been a state of contriving and struggle. In Zen this is self-discipline; in Shin it is coming to an acute awareness of one's insufficiency through a previous attempt at self-discipline. It is difficult to see how the Shin experience could be fully appreciated unless, like Shinran, one had first tried the *jiriki* way. The danger of continuing in the jiriki way is that one may so easily become a victim of spiritual pride, expecting to *make* oneself into a Buddha; the danger of the *tariki* way is that the experience may come so easily that its true meaning is unseen and its force unfelt.

Spiritual freedom, however, involves much more than going on living exactly as you have lived before. It involves a particular kind of joyousness, or what the Buddhists term bliss *(ananda)*. It is the discovery that to accord with the universe, to express the Tao, one has but to live, and when this is fully understood it becomes possible to live one's life with a peculiar zest and abandon. There are no longer any obstacles to thinking and feeling; you may let your mind go in whatever direction it pleases, for all possible directions are acceptable, and you can feel free to abandon yourself to any of them. Nowhere is there any possibility of escape from the principle of nonduality, for "you yourself as you are—that is Buddha Dharma." In this state there can be no spiritual pride, for union or identity with the Buddha principle is not something achieved by man; it is achieved for him from the beginning of time, just as the sun has been set on high to give him light and life.

Yet, in the life of the spirit, it is much harder to receive than to give; it is often such a blow to human pride to have to accept from Amida, God, or life what it would be so much more distinctive to achieve for oneself. In Shin terms, we should say that the meaning of freedom is that you can think any kind of thought, be any kind of person, and do any kind of thing without ever being able to depart from Amida's all-embracing love and generosity. You are free to do as you like, and also as you don't like, to be free and to be bound, to be a sage and to be a fool. Nowhere are there any obstructions to spiritual activity. At the same time, there is an intense awareness of the joy of that activity; one feels impelled to exercise it and feel the ecstasy of its abandon, much as we imagine a bird must feel high up in the air, free to soar up, to swoop down, to fly north, south, east, or west, to circle, climb, tumble, or hover. For "the wind blowest where it listeth, and thou hearest the sound thereof, but canst not tell whence it com-eth nor whither it goeth. Even so is everyone that is born of the spirit." Or, in the more matter-of-fact language of a Zen teacher, "There are no by-roads, no cross-roads here. All the year round the hills are fresh and green; east or west, in whichever direction you may have a fine walk."

There remains the moral problem. To a superficial under-standing the freedom of nonduality seems to be an invitation to libertinism of the most flagrant kind. In terms of philosophy, the Mahayana sutras state very frankly that the principle of nondual-ity is beyond good and evil, and that its attainment has no essen-tial connection with morality. And morality here includes all kinds of works, both social and spiritual. Certainly the sutras speak of *sila,* or morality, as one of the necessary stages, but sometimes it seems as if sila were advocated simply as a safeguard against misuse of the enormous, amoral power of supreme knowledge. Thus the *Lankavatara-sutra* says:

> In ultimate reality there is neither gradation nor continuous succession; [only] the truth of absolute solitude *(viviktadh-arma)* is taught here in which the discrimination of all the images is quieted. . . . But [from the absolute point of view] the tenth stage is the first, and the first is the eighth; and the ninth is the seventh, and the seventh is the eighth . . . what gradation is there where imagelessness prevails?*

In yet another passage we read:

> Some day each and every one will be influenced by the wis-dom and love of the Tathagatas of Transformation to lay up

*Yeh-hsien, D. T. Suzuki, *The Training of the Zen Buddhist Monk* (Kyoto, 1934), 83.

a stock of merit and ascend the stages. But, if they only realized it, they are already in the Tathagata's Nirvana for, in Noble Wisdom, all things are in Nirvana from the beginning.

An even stronger statement of the philosophy will be found in the *Saptasatikaprajnaparamita Sutra*:

> O Sariputra, to commit the offences is to achieve the inconceivables, to achieve the inconceivables is to produce Reality. And Reality is non-dual. Those beings endowed with the inconceivables can go neither to the heavens, nor to the evil paths, nor to Nirvana. Those who commit the offences are not bound for the hells. Both the offences and the inconceivables are of Reality, and Reality is by nature non-dual. . . . In the real Dharmadhatu (Realm of the Law) there is nothing good or bad, nothing high or low, nothing prior or posterior . . . Bodhi (Enlightenment) is the five offences and the five offences are Bodhi. . . . If there is one who regards Bodhi as something attainable, something in which discipline is possible, that one commits self-arrogance.*

Here, besides an unequivocal statement of nonduality, there is again an example of *tariki* psychology, speaking of the arrogance of striving to attain Bodhi by discipline.

Mahayana does not disguise the fact that its wisdom is dangerous and we know that monks of the jiriki schools are subjected to rigid disciplines just to precondition them against abuse of knowledge, which is unfortunately a fairly frequent occurrence. But it would seem that such abuse is only possible when the expe-

*Saptasatika*, pp. 232–34. D. T. Suzuki, *Essays in Zen Buddhism*, Vol. 11, pp. 251–52 n.

rience of freedom is feebly appreciated or improperly understood. Oddly enough, although the experience itself and the thing experienced (Tathata) is nondual and beyond good and evil, the result of a truly deep experience is morality. Shinran speaks very strongly against those who make use of Amida's vow and then go on behaving as immorally as ever. He likens them to those who, because they have found an antidote to a poison, just go on taking it. But this is rather a negative way of looking at the problem. From the positive standpoint, Shin would say that Amida's compassion for us and all other beings, when realized, calls out a corresponding compassion in ourselves.

In terms of philosophic Mahayana, we should say that, having understood that we and all creatures are Buddhas, we therefore treat them with the reverence due to the Buddha principle.

A second factor which makes for morality is the gratitude felt for the freedom to be all of oneself, a gratitude so deep that men will often renounce some of that freedom as a thank-offering. Obviously there is more opportunity for this feeling of gratitude to grow when the Ultimate Reality is personalized in the form of Amida. From the philosophic standpoint there is no real ground for gratitude, because in nonduality there is neither giver nor receiver. Hence the danger of a merely philosophic understanding. But from the emotional standpoint there appears to be every reason for gratitude. In discovering freedom to be all of oneself one has a similar experience to the Christian forgiveness of sins; however black your soul, it is not outside the love of God, which is as omnipresent as God Himself, and in this connection it is worth citing a remarkable passage from the work of a Catholic theologian:

> For we are never really outside of God nor He outside of us. He is more with us than we are with ourselves. The soul is less intimately with the body, than He is both in our

bodies and souls. He as it were flows into us, or we are in Him as the fish in the sea. We use God, if we may dare to say so, whenever we make an act of our will, and when we proceed to execute a purpose. He has not merely given us clearness of head, tenderness of heart, and strength of limb, as gifts which we may use independently of Him when once He has conferred them upon us. *But He distinctly permits and actually concurs with every use of them* in thinking, loving or acting. This influx and concourse of God as theologians style it, ought to give us all our lives long the sensation of being in an awful sanctuary, where every sight and sound is one of worship. *It gives a peculiar and terrific character to acts of sin.* . . . Everything is penetrated with God, while His inexpressible purity is all untainted, and His adorable simplicity unmingled with that which he so intimately pervades, enlightens, animates and sustains. Our commonest actions, our lightest recreations, the freedoms in which we most unbend—all these things take place and are transacted, not so much on the earth and in the air, as in the bosom of the omnipresent God. [Italics mine]*

There are important points in which Faber's words diverge from Mahayana philosophy, for, in Christianity, God is essentially Other. But, insofar as doctrine is a symbol of inner experience, I can see no important difference between the inner feeling suggested by Faber's words and the inner feeling of Mahayana Buddhism, especially in the Amidist cults. Thus the experience of freedom or Enlightenment is like discovering an immeasurably precious jewel in one's littlest acts and lowest thoughts. One discovers it where all jewels are first found—in the depths of the earth, or lying in the mud. Those who appreciate jewels do not leave them there; they lift them up from the depths, polish them,

*F.W. Faber, *The Creator and the Creature* (Baltimore, 1853), 65.

place them on velvet or set them in gold. This polishing and adornment is our symbol of morality, the expression of our joy and gratitude in realizing that: "This very earth is the Lotus Land of Purity, And this very body is the body of Buddha."*

It is here interesting to note that considerable importance is given to worship in the Zen school which, philosophically, is the most inconoclastic form of Buddhism. Perhaps there is a clue to the apparent inconsistency of worship and nonduality in the following incident from the *Hekigan-roku*:

> Huang-po (Japanese, Obaku) stated, "I simply worship Buddha. I ask Buddha for nothing. I ask Dharma for nothing. I ask Sangha for nothing." Someone then said, "You ask Buddha for nothing. You ask Dharma for nothing. You ask Sangha for nothing. What, then, is the use of your worship?" At which remark, Huang-po gave him a slap on the face!†

The Buddhist feeling of worship and gratitude is most notably expressed, however, in the Bodhisattva-ideal, based on a profound intuition of the basic unity of all creatures and things. Those who, having attained Enlightenment, do not become Bodhisattvas, helpers of the world, are termed *pratyeka-buddhas*, which, in Mahayana philosophy, is almost a term of abuse. They are not willing to share their experience of freedom with their other selves, and, strictly speaking, Enlightenment is no Enlightenment unless it is shared and circulated. It is no one's property, and those who try to possess it for themselves do not understand

---

*From the *Song of Meditation* by Hakuin (1683–1768), one of the most famous Japanese Zen teachers.
†I follow the version of Kaiten Nukariya. Cf. his *Religion of the Samurai*, p. 96. Buddha, Dharma, and Sangha (the Buddha, the Law, and the Order of monks) are the Three Refuges (*trisharana*) taken by all Buddhists.

it. Service, morality, and gratitude are our response *as men* for a gift to which we cannot respond *as Buddhas*. The Buddha-principle is beyond morality, but not so the human principle. From the standpoint of nonduality, these two principles are one; yet what is so often overlooked in the study of Mahayana is that from the *same* standpoint they are two. For nonduality excludes nothing; it contains both unity and diversity, one and many, identity and separation. Japanese Buddhism expresses this in the formula *byodo soku shabetsu, shabetsu soku byodo*—unity in diversity and diversity in unity. For this reason, philosophically, morally, and spiritually, Buddhism is called the Middle Way.

# Tomorrow Never Comes

WHEN WE SAY THAT ALL THINGS IN THE UNIVERSE are the creative activity of God, this is really like putting legs on a snake or painting the reflection on a mirror. It is not to be compared to seeing that activity as it is, although we say that it is God's activity to draw attention to it in a particular way. But the trouble is that people spend so much energy looking for the God that they fail to see the activity, which is surely a sad state of affairs. What is this activity? The rivers flow; the flowers bloom; you walk down the street. Really we should need to say no more than this, but it is sometimes called the activity of God to point out a certain understanding to the sort of person who might retort, "The rivers flow; the flowers bloom; you walk down the street—so what?"

So what? Well, what else are you looking for? Here is someone who eats out the grocer's store and still complains that he is starving. But the word and concept *God, Brahmin, Tao* or what you will, was really introduced for such unappreciative stomachs. It is a way of emphasizing actual life to draw attention to it in much the same way as we underline words or put them in italics. Thus we call the universe the activity of God to induce the so-whatter to pay some attention and reverence to it, because he always bolts his life instead of rolling it appreciatively round his tongue. He always thinks of the second and third pieces of cake while he is eating the first, and thus is never satisfied with any of them, and ends up with a thoroughly disordered digestion. This is called the vicious circle of having lunch for breakfast, or living for your future. But tomorrow never comes.

The snow is falling on the windowsill. Is this the activity of God? Maybe. But if anyone watches it *in order* to see God he will surely be disappointed. "No man hath seen God." No, and in looking for God he may fail to see the snow. "Thou art Brahman!" But if you look in yourself *in order* to find Brahman, you will be very disappointed indeed. Yet all this trouble has started because people have taken a simple device much too far. The idea of God is a finger pointing the way to Reality, but when people try to join God and Reality, to identify the one with the other, to find the former in the latter, they are trying to join together two things that were never in need of being joined. This is like trying to make the eyes see themselves.

Yet how do we arrive at the state where to watch the snow falling is so much one with God that we need no more introduce God than put red paint on the roses? Whence all this hurry to arrive at a state? Are you not already watching the snow? Are you not already face-to-face with the eternal mystery? Take it easy for a while; just watch the snow falling or the kettle boiling, and not so much hurry. What's wrong with watching the snow or the kettle that anyone should want to arrive at a state? It is possible that any ordinary moron can do this just as well, and why not go him one better? How splendid is his ignorance! Like the stones, the grass, and the wind, he has Enlightenment without knowing it, and cannot appreciate his good fortune. Yet he, too, is a so-whatter, for he asks "So what?" when others go questing for God. He is not free to watch the snow because he can do nothing else, and especially because he does not appreciate his freedom.

But you are free to abandon yourself to actual life and to know that living in God is another name for this abandonment, for watching the snow and walking down the street. And you are free not only because you have once been a so-whatter, but also because you have been living in this abandonment all the time, though without knowing it. If you had actually to get into it, to arrive at a state of abandonment where you had not previously been, you would not be free for this would involve *going somewhere,* arriving tomorrow at a place where you were not yesterday. And tomorrow never comes.

You say you do not feel this abandonment right now. What do you expect to feel? It is not a feeling; it is feeling. It is not a thought; it is thinking. If it were a particular thought or feeling there could be coming into it and going out of it; but God is One and all-inclusive, and here there can be neither coming nor going, inside or outside. More than this, the great abandonment of Enlightenment does not depend even on feeling and thinking, consciousness or unconsciousness, living or dying. As the verse says:

> This you can not describe, nor paint,
> Nor yet admire, nor feel.

It is your real self, that has no hiding-place. Destroy the universe, and it remains. No, you can't feel it—but then how can you know anything about it at all? Because you can *use* it and feel its use, just as "the wind bloweth where it listeth, and thou hearest the sound thereof but canst not tell whence it cometh nor whither it goeth." What is it like to feel its use? This is told in another verse:

> Sudden the cold airs swing. Alone, aloud,
> A verse of bells takes wing. And flies with the cloud.

# What Is Reality?

PEOPLE OFTEN SAY THAT THEY ARE LOOKING FOR Reality and that they are trying to live. I wonder what that means?

Some time ago a group of people were sitting in a restaurant, and one of them asked the others to say what they meant by Reality. There was much vague discussion, much talk of metaphysics and psychology, but one of those present, when asked his opinion, simply shrugged his shoulders and pointed at the saltshaker. He was amazed to find that no one understood him, yet he had intended to be neither clever nor obscure. His idea was just to give a commonsense answer to the question, on the ordinary assumption that Reality is whatever exists. He was not understood because his friends, in common with many others, regarded Reality as a special kind of existence and Life (with a capital L) as a particular way of living. Thus we often meet those who talk about the difference between being a mere clod, a mere "animated stomach," and a *real* person; between those who simply exist and those who really live.

In Chinese philosophy Life is called *Tao,* and the Chinese speak of the wise man as one who realizes (makes real to himself) his accord and harmony with Tao. Therefore, it is asked whether Tao means Life in the sense of simple existence, or whether Tao is Life lived in a special way, lived faithfully, thoroughly, vitally and with a certain zest born of the joy of being alive.

The answer to this question depends solely on why it is asked. Let's see what the Chinese themselves say about it.

A pupil asked his teacher, "What is the Tao?" He answered, "Everyday life is the Tao."

"How," went on the pupil, "does one get into accord with it?"

"If you try to accord with it," said the teacher, "you will get away from it."

Indeed, we have all met those who are trying very hard to be real persons, to give their lives Reality (or meaning) and to live as distinct from existing. These seekers are of many kinds, highbrow and lowbrow, ranging from students of arcane wisdom to the audiences of popular speakers on pep and personality, selling yourself and making your life a success. I have never yet met anyone who *tried* to become a real person with success. The result of such attempts is invariably loss of personality, for there is an ancient paradox of the spiritual life whereby those who try to make themselves great become small. The paradox is even a bit more complicated than this; it also means that if you try, indirectly, to make yourself great by making yourself small, you succeed only in remaining small. It is all a question of motive, of what you want. Motives may be subtly concealed, and we may not call the desire to be a real person the desire to be great; but that is just a matter of words.

So many modern religions and psychologies make this fundamental mistake of trying to make the tail wag the dog, which is what the quest for personality amounts to. Old-fashioned Christianity was never so stupid, for its aim was never to achieve greatness (or great personality) for man. Its aim was simply to serve God and ascribe all greatness to Him. But in these days so many people find themselves unable to believe in the Christian God, and His more abstract substitutes fail to inspire any genuine devotion and reverence.

So we return to the original question, "What, then, is Life; what is Reality, that it may inspire us with devotion?" If we regard it as a particular way of living or as a particular kind of existence and accord our devotion to *that,* what are we doing? We are revering its expression in great personality, in the behavior of those whom we consider "real persons." But here is the snag. When we revere real personality in others, we are liable to become mere imitators; when we revere it as an ideal for ourselves, here is the old trouble of wanting to make yourself great. It is all a question of pride, for if you revere Life and Reality only in particular types of personal living, you deny Life and Reality to such humble things as, for instance, saltshakers, specks of dust, worms, flowers, and the great unregenerate masses of the human race. We are reminded of the Pharisee's prayer, thanking God that He had not made him sinful like other men. But a Life, a Reality, a Tao that can be at once a Christ, a Buddha, a Lao-tzu, and an ignorant fool or a worm, this is something really mysterious and wonderful and really worth devotion if you consider it for a while.

The Buddhist scriptures say: "When every phase of our mind is in accord with the Buddha-mind, there shall not be one atom of dust that does not enter into Buddha-hood." For Life and Reality are not things you can have for yourself unless you accord them to all others. They do not belong to particular persons any more than the sun, moon and stars.

# The Birth of the Divine Son

*A Study of a Christian Symbol*

EVEN TO THE AGNOSTIC, THE STORY OF THE DIvine Incarnation must remain one of the most fascinating legends handed down to us out of the past. Though usually accepted as a Christian story, it is one of the oldest myths of the human race, something so embedded in the foundations of thought that no mere intellectual scepticism can remove it. For reason operates only on the surface of the mind, and however purely rational a man may suppose himself to be, when he sleeps he is caught unawares by the thoughts that he believes to have vanished. In his dreams the old myths will appear again, and prove that there is a region of the soul of which he knows nothing and over which he has no control. The power of the Catholic Church lies precisely in the fact that more than any other Western creed it enshrines these myth-symbols which stir the depths of thought and feeling. Scientific rationalism may alter the surface, may clothe the spirit in a different garment, may make it act another part. But the result is only *acting,* a pretence, an outward show, against which the inner being rebels and brings to pass those severe mental conflicts which estrange man from life.

The Church, however, proves so often inadequate to cure the spiritual disease of modern man because he finds it impossible to believe its exclusive interpretation of those ancient symbols. For those who *can* believe, the Church is satisfactory, less on account of that interpretation than on account of the symbols themselves. Whatever we may read into them, they seem to retain a power in themselves which no amount of misunderstanding can destroy. Thus the fallacy of modern scepticism is that in rejecting the Church's doctrines it has rejected the symbols as well, and so, if the expression is not too crude, has thrown out the baby with the bathwater. However, the reference to the baby is particularly apt, because what is perhaps the most important of these symbols is concerned with the baby, the Holy Child "conceived of the Holy Ghost and born of the Virgin Mary." The attention of the Church has often been drawn to the inconvenient occurrence of this same story in other and older religions, as for instance in the legend of Maya and the Buddha, and of Isis and Horus. Whereupon the learned fathers have resorted to somewhat lame replies, calling upon that *demon ex machina,* the Devil, and suggesting that he put the story in other religions to confuse the faithful. Or on the other hand they suggest that the Grace of God conveyed a certain portion of ultimate Truth to the heathen in order that they might be prepared for the Christian Revelation—a suggestion which is at once more shallow and more profound than its authors intend. For it creates the awkward and dangerous precedent of the Grace of God having been imparted by means other than the Church, and it seems just as much a preparation for the conversion of the heathen as for the scepticism of science. And if the argument were followed to its logical conclusion, it would end at that very difficult question of the identity of God and the Devil, for what to one is a source of Grace is to another a source of Temptation.

But before approaching the essential meaning of the Incarnation, it is interesting to note several important and suggestive correspondences. In the third chapter of Saint John's Gospel, Jesus is reported to have said that if a man would enter the Kingdom of God he must be born again of Water and the Spirit. Further, in the first chapter of Genesis, it is said that before the creation of the world the Spirit moved upon the face of the waters. It seems to follow, therefore, that these two elements, water and spirit, are necessary to Divine Creation, whether it is the creation of a universe or of a son of God. Thus it is interesting to enquire whether these two elements were concerned in the birth of that particular Son of God who is called Jesus Christ. At once, in accordance with orthodox teaching, we find Spirit—the Holy Ghost. It cannot be entirely accidental that there is a close resemblance between *Mary* and *mare,* the Latin for "sea" (*Mary* is a Greek form), while other significant words which derive from the same Sanskrit root *ma-* are *Maya* (the mother of the Buddha, meaning also the world of form, of phenomena), *mater* (mother), and the English *matter.* In all ancient cosmogonies, water is the symbol of matter, which, in union with spirit, produces the world of form. And just as spirit is active and masculine, water is passive and feminine. Thus, figuratively, water is the mother of the world, and from this we may gather that the story of the Incarnation may have a large number of equally true meanings. On the plane of cosmogony, it represents the birth of the world from the union of spirit with virgin matter, the planting of the seed of life into untouched soil. But its most important meaning is concerned with the spiritual development of man, with the idea of the Second Birth, with the realization that through being born anew, unregenerate man can become Christ, Son of God and Son of Man.

Ignorance and spiritual darkness is the result of being involved in a dualism, a conflict between opposites, whether divine and human, self and the world, conscious and unconscious. This is the condition in which almost every man finds himself on awakening to self-consciousness. There is an opposition between ourselves and the universe in which we live and the society to which we belong, for again and again we find that the demands of life conflict with personal desires. Hence there is a tendency to draw everything toward ourselves, to set ourselves up in a stronghold and to carry off into its walls whatever things in life we particularly desire. It is as if one tried to select certain aspects of the character of one's wife, or child, or parents, separate them from the whole and preserve them in unchanging isolation. Or again, it is like trying to persuade the weather to be always fine and warm, or even more like taking a human body and separating the beautiful parts from the ugly with the result that both die. For this separation, this isolation of the self from life, can only produce misery and spiritual death. Apart from life, the self is as meaningless as a solitary note taken from a symphony, as dead as a finger cut from the hand, and as stagnant as air caught from the wind and shut tight in a room. The same may also be said of any person, idea, object, or quality which the self tries to grasp and keep for its own exclusive property. On the other hand, the converse of this position is equally unfruitful. If the self is altogether overwhelmed by the world or totally absorbed in God or in the community, then it is as useless as a body which is all one limb, as dull as a tune of one uninterrupted note (or of every conceivable note played in one general uproar), and as absurd as a picture which has neither any particular color nor any particular form.

But between these two opposites, the self and the universe, there may be a union—not a merging together as water might be mixed with wine, but a union as between man and woman in which both opposites retain their individuality and yet bear fruit in the form of a child. It is often thought that the object of mysticism is to reveal the identity of all separate things, to deny utterly all individual existence and to find the One Reality whose manifoldness of expression is only the result of illusion. But there is an old Buddhist saying: "To him who knows nothing of Buddhism, mountains are mountains, waters are waters, and trees are trees. When he has read the scriptures and understood a little of the doctrine, mountains are to him no longer mountains, waters no longer waters, and trees no longer trees. But when he is thoroughly enlightened, then mountains are once again mountains, waters waters, and trees trees." For before we can truly appreciate the changing individuality of things we must, in a certain sense, realize their unreality. That is to say, one must understand that not only oneself but all other things in the universe are meaningless and dead when considered by themselves, as permanent, isolated, and self-sufficient entities. Unless related to the whole, the part is without value, and it is just this relating of the part to the whole, or rather, this realization of an already existing relationship, which is the union whereof the Holy Child is born.

Just as the husband must, if he in fact loves, receive his wife to himself and accept her wholly, at the same time giving himself completely to her, so must man accept the world and give himself to it. To receive the universe into oneself, after the manner of some "mystics," is simply to become inflated with the conceit that one is God and so to set up yet another opposition between the mighty whole and the degraded part. To give oneself utterly and slavishly to the world is to become a spiritual nonentity, a mechanism, a shell, a leaf blown by the winds of circumstance. But if the world is received and the self given at the same time, there then prevails that union which brings about the Second Birth. In this state alone is it possible to appreciate life in any real sense, to accept with love, gratitude, and reverence what is pleasing in other creatures together with what is not, through the knowledge that joy is unknown without sorrow, life without death, pleasure without pain. More than this, pain and death are not accepted simply *because,* by contrast, they make life and pleasure, but also because they are an integral part of a Greater Life and a Greater Pleasure. The Greater Life is more than life as opposed to death as a melody is more than sound; it is rhythmic presence and absence of sound in which silence and the ending of notes are just as important as their playing. It is not a question of merely tolerating the pause for the sake of the note, unless we may also say that it is tolerating the note for the sake of the pause. For just as little could be more hideous than an eternity of sound or an eternity of silence, so there is little to choose between an eternity of life and an eternity of death. But there is an alternation, a rhythm, a variety in things, as it were, a universal symphony. And this symphony is the Child of the Father, Sound, and the Mother, Silence.

Thus when we say that out of the union between self and life (or the world) there is born the Christ, we mean that man rises to a new center of consciousness which is neither in himself alone, nor in the world alone. Instead, he becomes centered in the harmony which results from the giving and receiving from the one to the other. Indeed, this center already exists whether he knows it or not, for no two opposites can exist unless there is a relation between them. And this relation, the Child, is Meaning, or what Keyserling calls *significance* and the Chinese term *Tao,* just as the child gives a meaning, a *raison d'être,* to the two opposites man and woman. In this sense the child is truly "father to the man" and Christ truly one with the Father. For what is mere substance, mere energy, mere whole, mere part, mere world, mere self? Each taken by itself is no more than an instrument, a tool, a lifeless quantity which the *Tao* brings together and shapes after its own meaning; indeed, without that meaning they could not exist at all. As to meaning itself, it cannot be described; it can only be experienced, and only experienced when there is such love between oneself and the world that what each makes together is more than either, just as to husband and wife the child is more than themselves.